To David Maclagan with great respect not least for his erudition.

Alec Jenner

September 1993

Schizophrenia

A Disease or Some Ways of Being Human?

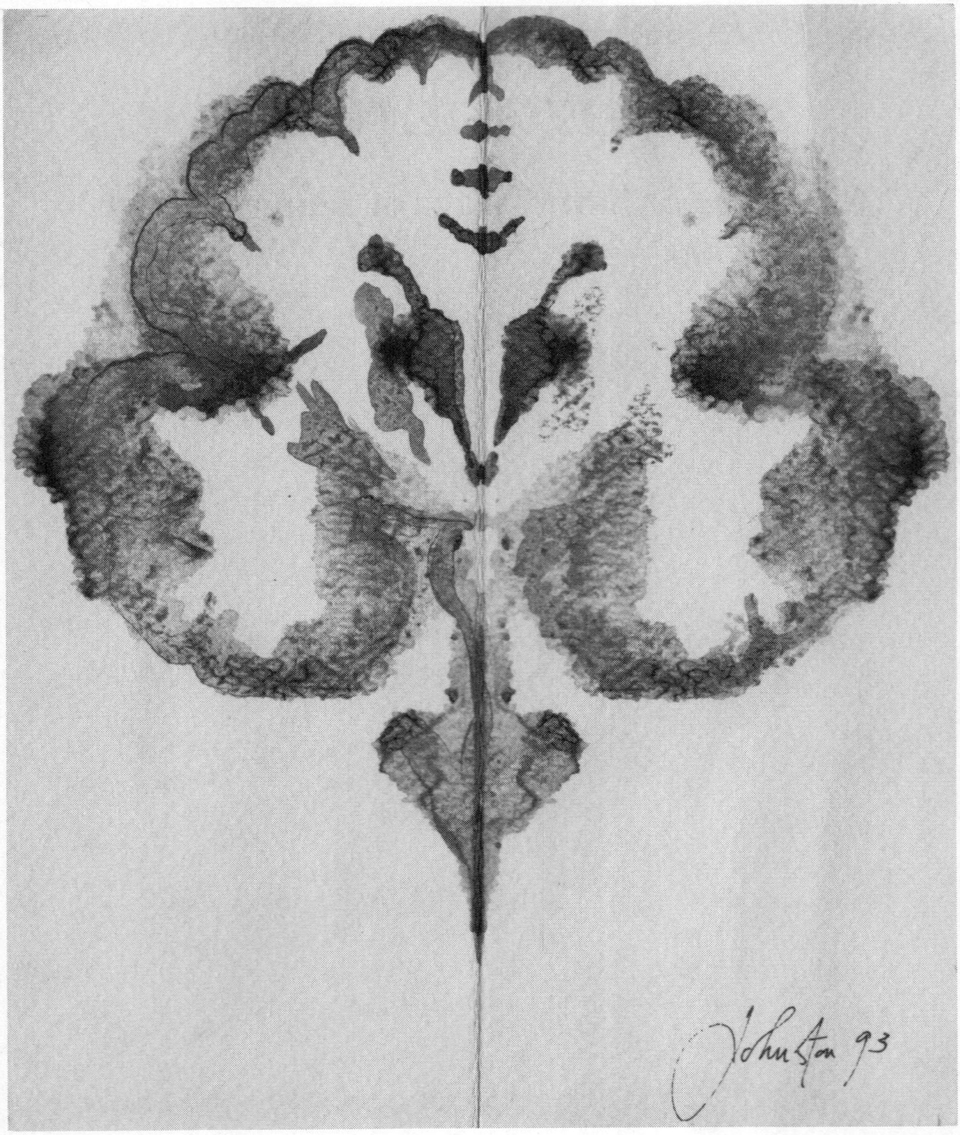
Johnston 93

Schizophrenia

A Disease or Some Ways of Being Human?

F.A. Jenner
Antonio C.D. Monteiro
J.A. Zagalo-Cardoso
&
J.A. Cunha-Oliveira

Foreword by Anthony Clare

Dedicated to Barbara, Dina and Joanna,

our long-suffering wives

Published by Sheffield Academic Press Ltd
343 Fulwood Road
Sheffield S10 3BP
England

Typeset by Sheffield Academic Press
and
Printed on acid-free paper in Great Britain
by The Charlesworth Group
Huddersfield

British Library Cataloguing in Publication Data

Schizophrenia: Disease or Some Ways of
Being Human
I. Jenner, F.A.

ISBN 1-85075-401-2

CONTENTS

FOREWORD

Initially I felt this was not going to be a book which I could in any way endorse. I started out believing that schizophrenia or the schizophrenias are probably best categorised as disease and to a very large extent I still hold such a view. But, as I read on through the book, I found myself agreeing with many of the central arguments—that we suffer from one of the strongest motives in the modern era, namely the desire to explain everything or rather explain everything away, that the ability to understand a patient's predicament, behaviour and utterances depends to a very great extent on psychiatrists' imaginative powers and also on their commitments to their patients and that there are good reasons for believing that when it comes to making sense of the process we call schizophrenia there are several roads to travel. This book indicates the choice of roads and combats the tendency for one road, be it biological, social or psychological, to be classed as the main thoroughfare.

Christian Scharfetter's observation (p. 38) summarises the book's main contention. The subject matter of psychiatry must indeed be the human being in toto, in the context of his or her life story. We get to know this subject matter only if we take the patient seriously and proceed with care towards an understanding of his or her condition. When we approach in this way those whose lives have gone badly, a psychiatric examination need not be a 'degradation' ceremony.

I found this book enormously provocative, challenging, compassionate and generous. In many ways, it is a welcome antidote to a certain mindlessness identifiable in modern psychiatry and warned against by Eisenberg, and a necessary reminder that psychiatry is indeed about holding the entire individual—brain and mind, body and psyche—in some cohesive whole. This book moves the argument about schizophrenia on from Laing's view of it as a willed statement of dissent and Szasz's notion of it as deliberately chosen deviance, and manages to mount a plausible case for regarding it as an understandable, if pathological, response to the vicissitudes of living. This book avoids labelling, stereotyping and scapegoating. While many contemporary psychiatrists will find much in the book with which to disagree they should read it for it serves to remind them and us that for all the current enthusiasm concerning brain research and biological advances, the schizophrenias remain one of modern medicine's most intractable enigmas and in the circumstances we would do well to approach the issue with a degree of open-mindedness and even humility if we are to avoid the bias, errors and mistaken assumptions of our predecessors.

Anthony Clare
Dublin

PREFACE

Schizophrenia remains an important mystery. It significantly destroys the lives of nearly one per cent of the world's population and devastates many families. But what is it?

This book holds that it is a modern word for much madness, and great care is necessary before describing it as a homogeneous condition. Classical psychiatry, clumping people together and using statistical techniques, tends to conclude that there is a genetic defect, often added to by birth injuries. This makes those people with damaged brains sensitive to interpersonal emotional intrusiveness. From the latter they can be protected by major tranquillisers, and many theories have been propounded based on the chemical effects of the drugs. The drugs are, however, double-edged swords, producing dulled people who may also have difficulties with movement. Not surprisingly, chemical interference with as complicated a machinery as the brain can hardly be expected to do only what is intended.

It is justified to try to support and advance this approach to the problem. Nevertheless, this book is one influenced by a tradition that attempts to defend human beings from reductionist and mechanistic assumptions. It would not be adequate simply to insist that human beings are different from computers or electro-chemical machines, the workings of which can be adequately explained in the language of the very successful nineteenth-century sciences. The history of Western European thought seems to belie that tendency to separate biology from chemistry. This book, therefore, while unashamedly confessing an acceptance of mystery, tries to discuss the findings of the natural scientists in their own terms.

There is, in particular, an insistence that confident physical explanations have been repeatedly postulated. At times we ourselves have accepted them. Time and again, however, what seemed scientifically proven has had to be rejected. Naturally we do not want to insist that nothing could nor will be found in brains which is really relevant. Our case is that interpersonal factors obviously matter, and hence the detailed lives and fears of people deserve closer scrutiny. That does sometimes make madness understandable. In due course, some of us hope to present such life stories, although we do not wish to pretend the problems can be simply solved.

Without being creationists, we are interested in the assumptions behind much of biology about consciousness as a product of blind chemical forces.

Much that science discovers must be within the language which it uses. It cannot find purpose in the universe as long as it insists on looking for mechanisms, and asking for more money when it cannot find them. It may be that thoughts will be shown to be supervenient (the other side of the coin) in relation to brain processes. To us it seems more likely that advancing knowledge will lead to changes in the whole language of science, and also the assumptions of scientific workers. Physicalism, which is now such a dominant view of modern philosophers could, like earlier ideologies, begin to look rather different. Philosophy, fearful of science, does often kowtow to it.

It is frequently thought that references to fundamental physics merely obscure many issues in psychology and biology. However, in this book we use such references to show how extrapolations of ideas, even from classical Euclidean geometry, come unstuck as absolute truths. The enormous amount of work needed to produce a rapprochement between chemistry and psychology will, we assume, change future centuries' views of reality. It is often our view of reality which the so-called schizophrenic rejects. Perhaps our willingness to be considered mad ourselves helps them and helps us to understand the strange others who reject common sense. Their rejection of accepted views leads to their own disenfranchisement (they have no valid votes) because they lack a certain 'healthy' degree of necessary social complicity. It is then a vicious circle set in motion which can destroy some of them.

We do not feel such people can be made well by logical arguments. The whole of our enterprise is an attempt to emphasise the degree to which devotion to being logical is a cover for what we are behind shutters—emotional and human. We all need a congenial place at the table, our views are often held for our own comfort. Even becoming an expert serves a human need for significance.

F.A. Jenner
Sheffield

ACKNOWLEDGMENTS

The texts in this book originally appeared as follows:

Chetcuti, M., A.C.D. Monteiro and F.A. Jenner
'The Domestication of Art and Madness and the Difficulties for the Outsider', *Rev. Psiquiat. Depart. S. Mental* 7 (1985): 41-53.

Cunha-Oliveira, J.A.
'*Da instituição à inovação e da inovação à instituição (viagem de ida e volta através da psicose)*, tese apresentada à Faculdade de Medicina da Universidade do Porto para obtenção do grau de Mestre em Psiquiatria, Porto, 1989.

Jenner, F.A., A.C.D. Monteiro and T.J.G. Kendall
'La esquizofrenía como problema en los Años 90', *Psicopatología* 4 (1984): 1-12.

Monteiro, A.C.D.
The Concepts of Understanding and the Schizophrenia Problem (PhD thesis, University of Sheffield, 1983).

Monteiro, A.C.D., and J.A. Zagalo-Cardoso
'Que "base genética" para a "esquizofrenia"?', *Rev. Port. Pedag.* 20 (1986): 179-201.

Monteiro, A.C.D., and J.A. Zagalo-Cardoso
'A investigação neurobiológicae o problema da casualidade na "esquizofrenia"', *Rev. Port. Pedag.* 21 (1987): 119-50.

Jenner, F.A., A.C.D. Monteiro and D. Vlissides
'The Negative Effects on Psychiatry of Karl Jaspers's Development of *Verstehen*', *Journal of the British Society for Phenomenology* 17: 52-71.

The English edition was typed by Mrs E. Isles and the references collated by Jane Allen-Brown and Debbie Sutton. We are indebted to them.

THE AUTHORS

F.A. Jenner
Professor of Psychiatry, University of Sheffield; Head of Department of Psychiatry, Royal Hallamshire Hospital, Sheffield, UK (1967–1992); Honorary Director of the Medical Research Council Unit for Metabolic Studies in Psychiatry, Sheffield (1967–1979)

Antonio C.D. Monteiro (1947–1987)
Professor of Psychiatry, University of Oporto, Portugal

J.A. Zagalo Cardoso
Senior Lecturer, Faculty of Psychology, University of Coimbra, Portugal

J.A. Cunha-Oliveira (Chapter 8)
Psychiatrist, St Clara Health Centre, Coimbra, Portugal

Manuel Chetcuti (Chapter 1)
Head of the Department of Fine Art, The Norfolk Institute of Art and Design, Norwich, UK

Chapter 1

The Domestication of Art and Madness and the Difficulties for the Outsider

(written with Manuel Chetcuti)

In reality the unique critics of art and literature
ought to be the psychiatrists; although they are as
ignorant about these issues and as remote from them,
and about what they call science as other people,
nevertheless when faced with mental disease they have
the competence that our judgment says they have.
No body of human knowledge can be built on any other bases.

Fernando Pessoa

THIS CHAPTER represents the result of discussions between psychiatrists and an artist. It presumes that there is general agreement that much of what is called successful art gives us a way of perceiving things differently. While there may be no logic of art, there are still historical factors. It is probably impossible to jump completely out of one historical context and to change radically and simultaneously everything called form and content. To do so is to demand too much to be understood and appreciated by contemporaries. The changes (advances?) are often achieved by 'speaking' to a small coterie who grasp or know the language.

But what in the language is one able to talk about? The answer seems to be about the very mystery behind being and the fact of experiences. The existence and nature of our own experiences we know perfectly well but there are associated mysteries somehow way beyond possible scientific explanations. While it is conceivable that in time there could be an explanation of art in terms of cerebral mechanisms, evolutionary theories and experimental psychology, this book is written assuming that it is unlikely. Instead it is suggested that there is something ineffable behind experience and aesthetics. Having a commitment to that might illuminate thoughts about psychoses.

Acceptable art is perceived as being significantly influenced by the genre of the period. Acceptable beliefs are similarly dependent on a degree of complicity with the common sense of periods. Attempts, though, to grasp what can be learnt by applying thoughts of students of art to the problems of psychiatry can often be impaired by being excessively iconoclastic towards psychiatry and romantic to the patient. There can be a failure to grasp the devastation that much called madness accurately implies. The artist and the insane may be both preoccupied with that which exists beyond and between the words we use, and be able to show us much which we usually overlook. However, to write or to talk is to make a concession to what might be called *logos*, or *cogito*. In doing so, art and madness remain slippery words but are not synonyms—all competent speakers can use both concepts with significant discriminant success. With Wittgenstein (1953: 43) we may refrain from asking what words mean, showing instead how they are used, yet we cannot be absolute relativists. In a complicated way words are related to the world, even if significantly also coloured by the world of human intention. A pure world of things in themselves may not exist, or if it does we are probably incapable of knowing much about it. With it and ourselves we create realities (Bachelard 1968).

Works of art, however innovative, have to be decodable in order to be understood and evaluated, and to do so a 'language' is required. In climbing a mountain to new heights one always requires one foothold to find the next. This is also true of all forms of communication languages; private languages are partially impossible, they are like the attempt to kick a football with two feet at once. Artists and the insane may try to explore and describe new vistas or experiences, and certainly the word mad will tend to be used to describe the degree to which others fail to understand them (cf. for example, Jaspers 1913) or are left 'without a leg to stand upon'.

Many ordinary people see the madness of our institutions but live with effective complicity in the human socio-historical context from which they know they cannot escape; some are blinded by it, others are content within it, and some see it as sacred and unalterable. Those groups are not called mad or avant-garde. Those who seem to us to act so strangely against their own interests, often with lack of guile, are the people likely to be diagnosed especially if they declare ideas about their own special significance (worth or worthlessness), breaking the obvious rule of society that others must seem to matter. They will be called mad too if they report hallucinations, strange non-socially confirmable bases for perception (cf. for example, Schneider 1959). The diagnosis can also depend on their apparent perception that the world, that is, other people, is devious and against them. These states of loneliness are, however, usually at least as undesirable as broken bones and, while Laing (1960) may romanticise madness, and it is possible that it is a difficult stepping-stone to the enlightened side of the stream, that is a precarious assumption especially if it is based on the idea that there is a mystical world to discover, some kind of 'extra-human' reality beyond the social reality of the language of human consensus. We wish to recommend accepting mysteries but not the mystification of them.

While Wittgenstein (1953) is almost correct that we must live in the cage of language, and certainly we must write a chapter like this in a cage of words; nevertheless our behaviour, art, madness and experience are still significantly beyond words. The attempt to express the realities and experiences beyond words and to try to grasp the strangeness of being, as distinct from nothingness (see, for example, Sartre 1943 and Heidegger 1978), is what we call accepting and explaining mysteries. It is not mystification, but realisation of much which is a central reality of our lives as lived, something which is characteristically human and can almost be communicated.

Human consensus on what is desirable is almost achievable because we can communicate much of human experience and so we understand that heart failure, fractures and malignancy for example are bad, not in God's mind but in ours. Something similar is also true of paranoia, depression, schizophrenia and obsessional neurosis. These assertions about what is bad seem as true as the statements that Homer, Michaelangelo, Beethoven and Shakespeare were great artists. For an earwig, an elephant, a man from Mars, things may be otherwise, but for most people this seems so. We recall, to situate the problem clearly, a woman with such gross cardiac failure that she could hardly talk, but she was very successfully treated by mitral valvotomy (heart surgery) and then developed dermatitis artefacta (self-inflicted injuries). Cardiac failure can, therefore, be desirable! Madness (individual, 'clinical') too may be better than complicity with more undesirable kinds of madness (even if they happen to be enacted by large numbers of people). Pain is often irrelevant to the spiteful and proud.

Thomas Hobbes (1914) essentially saw suicide as impossible for men, even if their lives are drab and miserable sequences of events. He would have argued that he spoke for the vast majority. Very few of our statements are absolutely true but our socially agreed realities, like his statements, are often fairly valid and we may be bound to label some rejection of them by words like mad.

It is very important for us though, in view of what else we want to explore, to start by making it clear that we do not want to extol and favour the child who will not go to the party and enjoy it, or the one who goes and wrecks it. Much of that behaviour we must accept, and we do very much want to understand why it is necessary when not effective strategically. What too, we must ask, can be rearranged in the future to serve the needs of as many as possible? We in general must struggle to help the negatively alienated and difficult, we must be concerned for them but not necessarily admire them as we admire those artists who have had the ability to use their alienation positively. Nevertheless, we must try to understand what the mad may be telling us about the 'state of the world'.

Having made these points, we would like nevertheless to attempt to draw some parallels between those who are historically and commonly called mad and some artists. There do remain confusions about behaviour, which is variously referred to as mad, rebellious or plain awkward. The mad and the bad, the dissident and the outsider, also have the potentially disturbing power to affect our collective sanity or culture and that affects our responses. The successful, non-subscribing outsider, by the nature of his existence, subverts the status quo by proposing a view of the world that he insists must be processed through his antennae. This requires that the collective view of the world must be tested by his own empiricism. This is necessary to make personal sense of his historical inheritance. He cannot or will not accept a wholly practical dogmatism as an aid to 'successful living', when, as is usually the case, it is merely a generalised formula for our social convenience and for avoiding the mystery and pain of his being. He is essentially a non-believer, a deeply spiritual sceptic and iconoclast.

The madman, like the artist, is construed by us in terms of his difference from the rest of us, so construing ourselves as well as him. The outsider is perceived as a challenge to our beliefs and perceptions, like an incurable sore on the otherwise serene face of our culture. It may be that there is an inevitable conflict between society and the outsider, for is not our communal half-blind stagger towards a Utopia based on ideas like those of a Garden of Eden, that promises tranquillity and immutability, a condition more associated with the dead than the living? Must continuous spiritual revolutions, with the exception of those of Spinoza's (1962) view, chip away at the foundations of a predominantly mechanistic culture? It becomes a threat that must be dealt with. Mysteries which cannot readily be explained are not pursued with alternative processes but are ignored, or worse they are pursued more vigorously with the same discredited criteria. They are relegated to a dark cupboard, only problems are entertained. It may be considered foolish to look for a black cat in a dark room when there is not a cat in there, but what is it if, when in pursuit of the non-existent cat, we chorus 'I've got it, I've found it'? Professor Donahue (1982: 3), the Henry James Professor of Letters at New York University, put forward the notion under the title the 'zealots of explanation', that we are ceasing to confront works of art directly through the image or object produced by the artist. We use instead the trivia that surrounds the activity as a substitute for understanding. This substitution of autobiographical anecdote enables us to side-step the more trying confrontation with the nature of the inherent message or mystery that the image or object may contain. 'I want to talk', Professor Donahue says 'about the arts in relation to the mystery that surrounds them, not as a problem to be cleared up but as the very condition in which they appear at all; in that sense mystery is to be acknowledged not resolved or dispelled.' It has become a scandal to talk of mystery, it appears to be a pretentious claim upon profundity as if the only situation worth talking about defeated every reasonable attempt to deal with it, but we want to reinstate mystery and to distinguish it from mere bewilderment or mystification. One of the strongest motives in modern life is to explain everything, and preferably to explain it away. The typical mark of modern critics is that they are 'zealots of explanation'. They want to deny the arts their mystery and to degrade mystery into a succession of problems, but the effort is perverse. The philosopher, Gabriel Marcel (1949: 69), has distinguished a mystery from a problem in this way. 'A problem' he says 'is something which bars my passage. It is before me in its entirety—a mystery is something in which I find myself caught up and whose essence is then not to be before me in its entirety.' This goes some way in helping to understand what we mean by domestication of the artist-outsider. We deliberately, if subconsciously, address ourselves to those problems inherent in the act to which we are fairly sure we already have the answers. Ah yes, he is a cubist or surrealist, or some medical term like a schizophrenic, which attempts to describe a state of mind. We use labels in order to side-step involvement. We need the critic and the doctor to provide us with the means to avoid the scandal. We do not use these devices as an affirmation—that we know what it means. We use them in order to avoid the discomfort of having to delve too deeply into what it might mean to us. One could say that the critic, like the psychiatrist, is not there to help us understand but through prescriptive explanation they help us to domesticate the terror of the mystery therein.

The mad, the rebellious, the dissident and the subversive artist provoke a common response from organised society. The realisation of their potential power brings about a crude consequence; the application of the full debilitating process of domesticating patronage. At this point it may help to describe a little more fully what we mean by domestication. The dictionary gives the following description: 'make fond of home', 'bring under human control' (with 'animals' in brackets), 'to tame, civilise' (with 'savages' in brackets). We would say that in this context it means to make you accept that which you may have already rejected. To bring under society's control and to tame and anaesthetise. Then, add to this the previously described technique of deliberately misunderstanding the rebel's intention, so as to deflect and minimise the power by concentrating on the trivial and irrelevant.

Michel Foucault (1963) notes the motto John Howard read over the door of the Hospital of Charity in Mainz: 'If wild beasts can be broken to the yoke, it must not be despaired of correcting the man who has strayed'. One of the ironic triumphs of the age of reason was to substitute the leper houses with places of confinement for a new category of outsider. The true intention was not medical but of a judicial nature, 'correction through confinement'.

Another example given by Foucault attributed to Pinel is of a monastic establishment in France where a 'violent madman' would be given an order say to eat his food, which if refused would be punished by ten strokes of a bull-whip. If, however, he was submissive and docile (who would not be after a few sessions with the bull-whip?) he was allowed certain privileges like eating at the table of his warder, but at the least transgression he was corrected with a heavy blow of a metal rod across his fingers. What we see here is not an attempt to raise the mad beast to the level of human, but to restore the man to what we would expect only of the animal in him, the animal in this case fully domesticated and the man's humanity denied. As Foucault says 'The animal is not silenced, it is the man who is abolished'.

These examples have their contemporary equivalents. It is surprising how often 'good' individuals and institutions are used as instruments of domestication through social control. A patient manifested thoughts which no-one agreed with (delusions) and spent most of his time on the ward mumbling jumbles of sentences (word salad). It was agreed that it was impossible to make any sense of what his wishes, desires or thoughts were (mad), but on one occasion he shouted at a rather stuffy and pompous staff member a sentence which contained an expletive and description of her, which is probably too crude to repeat here but which nevertheless amounted to a coherent and perfectly understandable, if rude, expression of his thoughts and feelings towards her. The sad outcome was that, rather than this act being taken as an indication of the man's lucidity, it was used as evidence against him, a confirmation of the diagnosis and an indication for his further deterioration. The one sentence that had made any sense was used as corroborating evidence of his madness. He was, of course, given more intensive treatment.

That apparently simple story has the ingredients of a classical case of domestication. The man, in the true Thomas Szasz (1984) sense, was an unwilling recipient of the treatment. The treatment was ordered because he did not make sense in the 'normal' way and with cruel irony the diagnosis was confirmed on the one occasion when he did make sense.

It is, of course, not the plain acts of individuals that we brand as mad or incomprehensible, it is whether we can discern an agreeable motive behind the act. *It is not so much that we need to perceive a motive as that we have to approve of it.*

This approval in reality is the giving of a moral blessing. The morality is derived from religious dogma. The authority to impose it comes from those pillars of the state—the judiciary, the organised church, the professions and the hierarchical family and the totalitarian political party.

This moral blessing is a disguised censorship every bit as crude as censorship generally is, but more subtle in its carrot and stick inducements to prescribed behaviour. The purpose is to uphold the institutions wherein our collective sanity is supposedly lodged. The result is a profound interference with the individual. The social establishment of religion, politics, science and art makes the censorship respectable in the eyes of the general public. The Catch 22 is that you must pursue your happiness through society's prescription. A question for all of us with power to consider is to what extent we are an extension of the power of the state?

Thomas Szasz described a situation which fits neatly into this socio-moral control aspect of domestication. The attempt by John Hinckley to assassinate President Reagan was considered mad because his motives were not approved of. You may remember that uppermost in Hinckley's mind was the desire to impress the actress, Jodie Foster. He was therefore considered mad because sane people do not shoot presidents for such a reason. No, sane people shoot presidents because they are politically motivated malcontents, preferably under the influence of a foreign or alien ideology. The fact that the result of the act in both cases may be the same does not come into it. For it is motives which are paramount here in the distinction of madness and sanity. Hinckley may have been mistaken (it may have impressed Jodie Foster but we doubt if it had the desired effect). He may have been a fool but was he mad? Is this further evidence of using a label in order to effect control? Hinckley was declared mad because the establishment's response to his declared motives were that they did not make sense. There was an attempt to neutralise him for his actions because they were dimly seen as a greater threat to the state because they were quite understandable! If you trivialise the office of president by putting your romantic aspirations first, then the whole panoply of the establishment's forces are powerless. The state invariably turns then to its priests of science—the moral arbiters who pronounce him mad, the ultimate weapon.

There are very interesting parallels in art, where the apparently incomprehensible is vigorously vilified. Works that are outside the prescribed groove are often labelled mad, insane, or heretical, the last description often being freely substituted for the first two. The more gentle observer who, while not understanding, may hold judgment in the belief that he may come to understand in time, is perpetuating the myth of a thing being ahead of its time. Of course, nothing is ahead of its time. We do have to confront acts, images and objects for which we may not have the readily available grammar for decodification, but in its time it surely is. The anger directed at newness—the 'shock of the new' as Robert Hughes puts it—is a similar anger that we reserve for all those acts which have the presumption to move out of the prescribed groove. Foucault in *Madness and Civilisation* wrote 'The simplest and most general definition of madness in the classical sense is delusion (*delire*)'. This word derives from *lira* (a furrow) so that deliro-delirium actually means to move out of the furrow.

The French word *delire* presents problems in English translation, as English more sharply distinguishes delusions, to which Foucault was probably meaning to refer, from delirium (delude is etymologically to mock, to deceive, to play) often somewhat misleadingly used in translations of *delire.*

The original meaning of *delire* (Fr.), *delirio* (Port. and Sp.), delirious (Eng.) is given moral overtones by the common sayings: 'leaving the straight and narrow', 'going off the tracks', etc., although Sauvages does redress the balance with his epithet that 'delirium is (delusions are) the dream of waking persons'. Here we are dealing with an extension of 'the shock of the new'. We have here the 'shock of the strange', the unfamiliar. Strangeness is flung in our faces without the ministration of its attendant apologists. The anger directed at the artist outsider is all the more curious when one realises that by far the most common complaint is that the act, image or object is unintelligible, that it has no meaning, that it flings a paint pot in the face of the public, that they are wild beasts—remarks levelled at the Fauves in 1905. They are also called mad, evil, hoaxers. How is it then that we get so enraged over a meaningless act if it has no meaning, no power. How and why does it have such an effect upon us?

It is the power of the strange and unfamiliar that enrages us most. It is the challenge to our view of reality that causes the discomfort. Those acts which are not recognisable induce the discomfort. They challenge our communal sanity. The greatest anger and rejection is reserved for those works and acts which have the effrontery to step outside of contemporaneous normality. There is special rejection for those who celebrate and deepen differences—our essentially scientific and mechanistically orientated culture expects its intelligentsia to be mystery-solvers, not purveyors of the 'awkward stuff'. This need to have mystery solved like a conundrum, to see man's intellect as a laser illuminating and destroying all before it, is to deny that the most intransigent mysteries are not before us but in us.

The public's and critics' reactions to the unacceptable and unfamiliar are illuminating. There is, for example, a great deal of evidence of individual and institutional shock regarding nudity. Painting and sculpture without the actual or metaphorical fig leaf has caused uproar among prudes and bigots, and while the notion of so-called obscenity is outside our intended scope, it is relevant to note that the defenders of our morals in the main claim they are protecting others from the proscribed images, objects or acts. It is not themselves who may be corrupted but children—the impressionable—the weak of mind. The moral vigilantes go to ludicrous lengths to 'protect' others from experiencing the same thoughts that they have. The 'Rabbits' Wedding Dance', an illustration in a children's book, was removed from open circulation in the southern states of America in 1959 because the boy bunny was black and the girl bunny was white. It was alleged to have an integrationist intent. A Florida editor reported: 'This is brainwashing, as soon as you pick up the book and open its pages you realise these rabbits are integrated'. The board of aldermen in Buffalo, New York, adopted a resolution to the effect that statuary in the Allbridge Gallery should either be draped or segregated. The censored statues were from the 'Golden Age of Greek Art', including the Venus de Milo, Apollo and the Venus de Medici. The Catholic bishop of the diocese felt that such action should be taken because the public exhibition of nudity was 'demoralising and harmful especially to the immature'.

He was, of course, not referring to himself but to others. An international exhibition of modern art held in New York in 1913 created 'public shock', 'press ridicule' and 'critical attack'. Paintings, prints and sculptures by the then new artists, some 400 works by, amongst others, Cezanne, Matisse, Gaugin, Picasso and Van Gogh, served to 'start riots' and 'alert vice squads'. The *New York Times* assessed the show as pathological and hideous. Further recorded comments when the exhibition moved to Chicago were 'the idea that people can look at this sort of thing without it harming them is rubbish'. The director of Chicago's Art Institute evaluated the cubist works in the exhibition as a 'toss-up between madness and humbug'. However, the balance was redressed somewhat by the observation of one commentator, who said that he felt that 'art was recapturing its own essential madness'. In a definitive statement of the Soviet party's credo in the late 1960s relating to 'freedom in the arts', it says: 'The arts must be a source of happiness and inspiration to the masses—it must enrich them ideologically and educate them morally'. Some happiness, some inspiration, what freedom? It would not help if the deviant artist moved to Spain for there works rejected for exhibition (at around the same time) by the National Ministry of Information were accompanied by the rejection notice: this work is too social and political for acceptance'. The double-speak is plain to see. 'Freedom in the arts' means toeing the party line; art is propaganda and the Ministry of Information informs you that this information is banned!

Here is a curious example of a view being censored on the basis of 'good' censorship. The following statement by a 16-year-old negro girl was struck out of the catalogue for the exhibition 'Harlem on my Mind' because it was deemed anti-Semitic. She had written: 'our contempt for the Jews makes us feel more American in sharing a national prejudice'. There are, of course, thousands more examples of attempts to reject, suppress or negate the new, unfamiliar or merely disconcerting. Perhaps one of the most chilling concerned the Florentine sculptor Pietro-Torrigiano, who was commissioned by the Spanish Duc d'Arco to make a sculpture of the Madonna. The duke and he, however, could not agree a price for the completed work so Torrigiano destroyed the piece. As a result he was brought before the inquisition in Seville, found guilty and condemned to death for *sacrilege*. The implications of his trial and sentence are breathtaking for if he was such a heretic how then was he able to make a work holy enough to be guilty of sacrilege?

A society without deviance—without art—is not being advocated, nor necessarily a more 'liberal' attitude towards the outsider. Whether the society is totalitarian and militarist or decadently liberal is not the issue at stake here. These opposite points of the historical social cycle have within them political and social consequences which are more effectively dealt with by political and social tools.

It is the relentless pursuit to concretise the mystery of our being which most effectively bars our passage. In our monolingual drive to construct an essentially Euclidean model of the universe we imply that all mysteries are merely problems and all problems can be solved with the right construct. Perhaps madness is the tyranny of inexpressible thought, which can however be made more meaningful and understandable. Art, therefore, could be seen as thought shared and made public—private language overcome, but nevertheless having an essentially mad element. For without that vital mad element art becomes merely descriptive, a comfort, a prop, an armchair rooted in the fashions of the time or propaganda supporting state power. We need the mirror the outsider holds up not in order to confirm who we think we are but to discover what we might be.

The painter and sculptor, Marcel Duchamp (1972), who profoundly affected our view of the world earlier in this century, subsequently gave up the practice of art. He said in an interview in 1963: 'In the final analysis I probably stopped performing as an artist because I did not want to become the victim of the integration of the artist into society'. The implication that domestication of the individual may be inevitable is plain to see. In that case resisting for as long as possible is the only strategy. Thomas Szasz's (1971) argument that the involuntary patient in psychiatry makes that practice an extension of the law has an attractiveness that the outsider may be foolish to welcome. For if at the end of the day all it means is a sort of benign neglect, or worse a eugenic neo-Darwinism, the application of the law of the survival of the fittest in human affairs, then he is merely substituting the misery of intervention with the morality of the jungle.

In our opening remarks we spoke of what we believed to be a confusion between madness and creativity—that labels are eagerly sought and incorrectly applied. Foucault (1963) says that 'madness is common to the language of art'. He does not say that it is the only thing common to it. Madness is not in the nature of the message but in the inexpressibility of the condition. Maybe, but the art of psychiatry, one ephemeral idiom in the history of the art of being human, itself requires us to reconsider professional structures and modes of reacting, how in fact to run our lives and our families and certainly to notice the strangeness of much of our logic and need to achieve conformity.There are some facts in the field, as there are in art; one can learn about the properties of drugs, pigments, compulsion and marble. If madness supplies the sublime impetus and is, as Foucault said 'contemporary with the work of art', then it is its combination with language that gives birth to the creative statement.

In treating the body that shows no lesion, are we like those of old, merely attempting to exorcise demons? For being unable or unwilling to change the world for the outsider, are we applying a false logic in trying to change him to suit the world? He is in fact an insider looking out. His madness in the end may be in having constructed a world he cannot describe to us.

Chapter 2

From a Critique of Karl Jaspers's Concept of Understanding to the Idiographic Approach to Schizophrenia

There are no words for the profound experience. The more I explain myself the less I understand myself. Of course, it isn't that everything is incommunicable in words, but that truth is living.

Eugene Ionesco

Introduction

THERE IS an influential strand in German philosophy which asserts that there are two types of knowledge. Using the first, one understands another person because one is human. Using the second type, one explains, for example, the illness or behaviour of the other because of one's scientific or medical knowledge. We understand jealousy or *Schadenfreude*; we explain the delirious state of the child with measles.

Karl Jaspers was not the first person to write a *General Psychopathology*, but he was by far the most influential. He was in particular very influenced by German understanding and debate. Perhaps it is helpful here to give a simple dramatis personae of other founders of German psychiatry. Emil Kraepelin delineated a condition called dementia praecox, and later Eugen Bleuler suggested schizophrenias as a better title. He used the plural to hedge his bets about homogeneity. That term was accepted. Kraepelin had emphasised by diagnosis the course of the illness starting around puberty and leading to a demented and destroyed person. Bleuler tried to combine psychoanalytical insights and association psychology in the concept and showed the outlook was not always so bad. As these criteria did not lead to categorical diagnoses, as do signs and symptoms in medicine, Schneider tried to identify the clear signs and symptoms—his so-called first and second-rank symptoms.

In this chapter the possibility (and ways) of understanding patients who have been diagnosed as schizophrenics is explored with the implications this has for treatment. To some extent we use Schneider's and Jaspers's ideas and refer to persons with specific symptoms that psychiatrists declare they cannot understand.

The concept of understanding is examined not only because it is an important criterion used by many in the diagnosis of schizophrenia but also because it is closely linked with very popular theories of the causes and nature of schizophrenic disorders.

There is a concept of schizophrenia applied by our colleagues to patients they perceive as unacceptably unintelligible. The majority of psychiatrists find these patients' ideas to be both beyond their own human understanding and also undesirable. That is what the word schizophrenia means semantically to many people. We are concerned then in how such conceptualisation affects clinical practice. Delusions, hallucinations, formal thought disorders and catatonic symptoms are striking and unusual to most of us but they are perhaps susceptible to meaningful interpretations within the context of patients' life histories. Some 'common-sense' views of the possibility of understanding other human beings' behaviour are liable to miss a great deal of its significance. We must not forget that before Freud many human actions now considered understandable (for instance, slips of the tongue and memory, obsessive and hysterical symptoms, etc.) were viewed either as inexplicable events or as pathological symptoms due to causal mechanisms located somewhere inside the central nervous system.

In our opinion, to understand or not to understand is an alternative very often decided not by the nature of the illness but by the power struggles fought amongst mental health professionals and between them and their patients. Time, concern and intellectual interest in our patients' problems are precious commodities which professionals have in short supply. Sometimes this is because they believe their training is of unique relevance, which debars the interference others. Status-seeking and other struggles also play a role.

The ability to understand depends to a great extent on psychiatrists' imaginative powers and also on their commitment to the patient. Hence, they have perhaps accepted too hastily the non-understandability of schizophrenics' symptoms and this was probably due to preconceived ideas that accommodated their own self-centred interests and allegiances.

In this study, therefore, an endeavour is made to demonstrate that psychiatrists have several ways of world making. Within these worlds they interact with their patients. As Nelson Goodman (1978: 2) wrote:

> Truth, far from being a solemn and severe master, is a docile and obedient servant. The scientist who supposes that he is single-mindedly dedicated to the search for truth deceives himself. He is concerned with the trivial truths he could grind out endlessly, and he looks to the multifaceted and irregular results of observations for little more than suggestion of overall structures and significant generalisations. He seeks systemisation, simplicity, generality, and when satisfied on these scores he tailors truth to fit. He as much decrees as discovers the laws he sets forth, as much designs as discerns the patterns he delineates.

Of course, our freedom is not absolute. We must be careful not to be driven by aleatory (throw of a die) choices of meaningless programmes of action. We have to take into account the state of the art at a given historical period and, on the other hand, the guesses we are entitled to make concerning schizophrenia cannot ignore what patients actually say or do. As Nelson Goodman (1978: 2-3) also wrote:

> While readiness to recognise alternative worlds may be liberating, and suggestive of new avenues of exploration, a willingness to welcome all worlds builds none. Mere acknowledgment of the many available frames of reference provides us with no map of the motions of heavenly bodies; acceptance of the eligibility of alternative bases produces no scientific theory or philosophical system; awareness of varied ways of seeing paints no pictures. A broad mind is no substitute for hard work.

We recognise, therefore, that in trying to understand patients diagnosed as schizophrenics we are making a bet and backing a horse in a race that is far from finished. For the time being, however, we think we have reasons for making this bet and trying to show that there are still several roads to travel and explore. If someone managed to produce a really convincing physical explanation for the experiences and behaviour of schizophrenic patients, we would certainly acknowledge the fallacy of our current approach. Yet, as Nelson Goodman (1978: 22) puts it: 'Discovering laws involves drafting them. Recognising patterns is very much a matter of inventing and imposing them. Comprehension and creation go on together.'

Jaspers and the Concept of 'Understanding'

In his *General Psychopathology* Jaspers considered schizophrenia an example of a psychotic process, an illness, that is most probably of organic origin and characterised by specific symptoms we could not understand in terms of patients' life events and biography.

Discussing what he called 'the basic problem of psychopathology: is it personality development or process?' (1913: 702), Jaspers wrote:

> The ununderstandable aspect of the process represents the limit of our understanding but this must be in the sense of a basic biological event and not in the sense of Existence itself which carries life on and gives it reality. The philosophical concept of Existence itself cannot be applied to concrete psychopathological investigations. If it is so applied it unavoidably loses its particular and profound meaning. The changes of human existence are not the changes of Existence itself. The transformation of the entire individual and his particular world by biological events which distort the course of his life and the transformation wrought by the unconditioned choices of Existence itself are two quite heterogeneous things. They do not lie in the same plane. The latter has no existence at all for the science of psychopathology. The intrusion of a process into the personality makes for madness, not for Existential freedom (1913: 705).

What does Jaspers mean by Existence itself? What are changes of human existence and how can they be differentiated from changes of Existence itself?

How can we distinguish (in the absence of independent criteria of validation) 'the distortions caused by biological events' from 'the transformations wrought by the unconditioned choices of Existence itself'?

We cannot blame Jaspers for having his own opinions but we must not regard his statements as overwhelming evidence in favour of the points he wants to demonstrate. In the absence of objective criteria for the diagnosis of schizophrenia (contrary, for instance, to the case of patients suffering from G.P.I. [General Paralysis of the Insane due to Syphilis], in whom Bayle [see Moore and Solomon 1934] was able to detect thickened meninges [the membranes covering the brain]), Jaspers cannot avoid a tautological kind of reasoning, defining schizophrenia by its 'ununderstandable' symptoms and considering these symptoms 'ununderstandable' on account of them being produced by an illness like schizophrenia. Language is a dangerous game to play. Most of the time we believe we are speaking about real things when in fact we are just using words for our own purposes. It is curious to notice that, although psychiatrists seem keen on correcting patients' mistaken concepts and self-defeating linguistic habits (see, for instance, Beck's [1976] 'cognitive psychotherapy', Ellis's [1973] 'rational-emotive therapy' and Kelly's [1955] 'personal constructs theory') they do not always appear so willing to examine (and reflect upon) their own 'language-games'.

It is interesting, however, to notice that even such an 'orthodox' author as Frank Fish (1966: 270) is forced to recognise that,

> whichever concept of schizophrenia we use, we must remember that our classification of non-organic psychoses is based on clinical features and not on aetiology. Until we can classify mental illnesses according to underlying neurophysiological and biochemical changes we can add nothing new to the arguments about the concept of schizophrenia and dementia praecox, which have occupied the best minds of psychiatry for the last seventy years.

It is equally interesting to point out that Jaspers himself could not help recognising that schizophrenic patients were different from patients with G.P.I. He wrote in *General Psychopathology* (1913: 576):

> but the psychic disturbances which occur in General Paralysis are of a radically different kind from those appearing in schizophrenia. In the one case it is as if an axe had destroyed a piece of clockwork—and crude destructions are of relatively little interest. In the other it is as if the clockwork keeps going wrong, stops and then runs again. In such a case we can look for specific, selective disturbances. But there is more than that; the schizophrenic life is peculiarly productive. In certain cases, the very manner of it, its contents and all that it represents, can in itself create another kind of interest; we find ourselves astounded and shaken in the presence of alien secrets, which in this sense cannot

> possibly happen when we are faced with the crude destruction, irritations and excitements of General Paralysis. Even when we have discovered the somatic processes underlying the psychoses there will always persist a profound contrast between the various psychoses and probably too an interest of quite a different order in their psychic aspects.

More instructive still are Jaspers's own doubts, perplexities and comments. In ch. 14 of *General Psychopathology* he wrote:

> The biological approach to cases is of great interest, especially when they do not allow, at any rate so far, any clear alternative between personality development and process. There are the rare so-called true 'paranoiacs', the progressive compulsive disorders, the 'insanities', without any elementary symptoms (false perceptions, thought disorder, primary delusions, passivity phenomena, thought withdrawal, etc.), yet perhaps with blocking and negativism (which one cannot always clearly distinguish from neurotic phenomena, the results of complexes). If in these cases there does not come across the break in the life-history the beginning of some known syndrome, diagnoses usually do not agree even in the hands of experienced specialists. What the one considers to be a neurosis or an anankastic development or psychasthenia, the other takes for a schizophrenia. Personality disorder or process, decidedly abnormal personality, or schizophrenic transformation of a previously quite different being are two diagnoses in opposition yet opposed in such a way that not only do difficult cases occur but, because of such cases, the basic concepts are themselves in question and their limitations constantly felt (1913: 705).

Despite his doubts and provisos, Jaspers decided to conclude this same chapter by emphatically declaring:

> The investigation of the basic biological events and the meaningful development of the life history culminates in a differentiation of the kinds of individual life: the unified development of a personality (based on a normal biological course through the age-epochs and any contingent phases) and the disruption of a life which is broken in two and falls apart because at a given time a process has intervened in the biological happenings and irreversibly and incurably altered the psychic life by interrupting the course of biological events.

In another passage of the same book he wrote:

> Irrespective of the difficulties in the individual case we still have to avoid extending understanding beyond the realm of the understandable. Something like a basic attitude in psychiatry is manifested here and hence there is a passion in the polemics. Connected with all the attempts to understand schizophrenia we find the tendency to deny the facts of the process in their specificity (1913: 706).

After reading Jaspers one cannot help asking: what facts? what process? what specificity? What does it mean to say that something is beyond human understanding? What stipulates (and how) the realm and limits of the understandable, beyond which we should not be allowed to go? In *Steps to an Ecology of Mind*, Bateson (1978: 193) puts forward a completely different view when he writes:

> Many writers have treated schizophrenia in terms of the most extreme contrast with any other form of human thinking and behaviour. While it is an isolable phenomenon, so much emphasis on the differences from the normal—rather like the fearful physical segregation of psychotics—does not help in understanding the problems. In our approach we assume that schizophrenia involves general principles which are important in all communications and therefore many informative similarities can be found in 'normal' communication situations.

Here it is worth briefly referring to Eugen Bleuler's (1911) ideas concerning the entity whose very designation derives from his research and writings. Although theoretically accepting Kraepelin's assumptions regarding the delineation of the clinical entity dementia praecox and the general downhill course of the illness, as well as Kraepelin's underlying notion that some organic alteration was at the root of the symptomatology, Bleuler presented a psychological theory for schizophrenia clearly inspired by Freud and the psychoanalytical school of thought. We must not forget Bleuler's oft-quoted adage while he was still trying to understand (and had newly coined the word) schizophrenias: 'The more hysterical the hysteria, the more schizophrenic the schizophrenia' (1911: 102). He called attention to the similarities existing between dreams and schizophrenic symptoms and compared his own concept of autistic thinking with Freud's concept of primary processes thinking. He wrote: 'The pathogenic complexes [in 'schizophrenia' that is] overpower and pervert the balancing impact of language'. Stierlin (1967: 999), in 'Bleuler's Concept of Schizophrenia: A Confusing Heritage', wrote:

> In emphasising that schizophrenic symptoms exaggerated normal experiences, that the psychological setting was all-important, and that there existed many abortive and latent forms of schizophrenia, Bleuler indeed threatened the very Kraepelinian edifice which he had set out to complete and underpin. That was the paradoxical result of his efforts. This result, when taken seriously, would have opened new and exciting perspectives. But for a long time it did not. The main reason for this lay with Bleuler.

Apparently, Bleuler became increasingly bogged down by the contradictions and attacks he himself had engendered, in contrast to Freud who disregarded his critics and pursued a lonely path of theory-building. Soon reminded by his colleagues that he was on slippery ground, Bleuler succumbed to the claims of the academic quarters. For example, in Fish (1964: 298) we read:

> Although there were outstanding exceptions, it is generally true to say that what German psychiatry gained in scientific accuracy (?) and clinical knowledge (?) it lost in humanity. The somatic neurological approach to psychiatry led naturally to a neglect of the psychological and social aspects of mental illnesses, which sometimes can be of much more importance in the treatment and general management of a patient than any hypothetical organic cause of his illness.

Stierlin (1967: 1000) wrote of Bleuler that,

> He became more and more insistent in claiming organic causes for the disturbance. Although we read in his textbook: 'We do not know as yet on what the pathological process is based', we learn immediately thereafter: 'In acute stages various kinds of changes in the ganglion cells are found. In old cases the brain mass is reduced a little; many ganglion cells, especially in the second and third layers, are changed in various ways; sometimes the fibrils of the cells and the axons look diseased. The glia is regularly involved; various changes of its cell varieties, increase of the small cells. There is a deposit of pigment and other catabolic materials, increase of the finer glia and other things besides'!

Bleuler's choice was after all a 'strategic' decision shaped by the academic establishment's *Weltanschauung* and endorsing Kraepelin's authoritative viewpoints. We must not forget that Kraepelin studied his clinical cases in the highly artificial and deforming context of the large mental hospital in Germany around the turn of the century. Patients (mainly psychotic) were observed and treated as scientifically interesting (and dangerous) objects presenting curious and bizarre psychopathological symptoms, obviously (?) produced by natural causes and therefore independent of understandable human reasons, as has been pointed out by Bleuler (1911). In a less certain mood in 1927, he even declared that there is no disease schizophrenia (see Laing 1978 and Rosenhan 1973). Science is never completely neutral and context free, and in its workings it is always possible to perceive the influence of our purposes and allegiances.

In 1918 Kretschmer described a 'sensitive and understandable approach to delusions of reference'. This involved a more psychodynamic approach to delusions. The reaction of Kraepelin and Jaspers, among others, to Kretschmer is an example of an academic political power struggle. Rasmussen (1978: 443) wrote:

> On the publication of Kretschmer's book, Kraepelin (and, still more, his pupils) adopted a somewhat reserved attitude because of the importance he ascribed to the course and the outcome when the validity of a disease entity is to be assessed, and in view of his working method he claimed that a long period of observation was necessary if it could be accepted as more than a symptom complex (Kraepelin and Lange 1927).

Jaspers (1973) foresaw that the book would come to occupy a permanent place in the history of psychiatry, but he could not accept that it would be feasible on the basis of an analysis of the environment, character, predisposition and experience to familiarise oneself, that is, to 'understand', how conflicts and affects could result in truly incorrigible delusions. The line of demarcation which, a few years previously, he had drawn in his book *General Psychopathology* between the understandable, the empathically comprehensible, and the fundamentally incomprehensible was not respected here. In subsequent editions of *General Psychopathology* he still did not accept *sensitiver Beziehungswahn* (sensitive delusions of reference) as a distinct disease entity, but assumed that most cases were actually benign schizophrenias of late onset.

Studying these controversies one gets the impression that the concept of understanding was never fully discussed and clarified, despite its solid reputation among successive generations of psychiatrists as a ready-made criterion for the diagnosis of schizophrenia. In fact, since the time of Jaspers, Kraepelin and Eugen Bleuler, this 'beyond human understanding' has reinforced hopes of simple biochemical explanations for schizophrenia (since 'scientific explanations' are required for those experiences which we as human beings cannot understand), and has been combined for the same purposes with statistically developed psychiatric nosologies, although we know that multivariate statistical methods cannot produce objective classifications (classifications are for purposes). Much has been made too of the separation of the form of the illness from the content of thoughts, one explicable and only the other understandable.

Curiously enough, the diagnosis of schizophrenia (and the selection of case material for sociological, pharmacological and biochemical studies in this field) is being made on the basis of symptoms which we are not able to understand, although it is obvious that knowledge of what we cannot understand cannot be more reliable than knowledge of what we do understand! If it is logically demonstrable that one of the commonest medical diagnoses of a chronic disabling disease depends on such criteria, surely it will pay to try to explore them in a more critical frame of mind.

The Concept of 'Understanding' and the 'Idiographic' Approach to 'Schizophrenia'

The concept of humanistic understanding, which we present in this book, is not a concretely verifiable one for which one could find objective limits and criteria. To assess its usefulness as a diagnostic and therapeutic tool in the clinical study of schizophrenia one is bound to depend on human intuition and imagination and also on willingness to accept the concept itself.

Jane Austen, Shakespeare, Thomas Hardy and Goethe knew nothing with confidence about people (despite their deserved reputation as inspired painters of the human soul), but psychiatrists' current concepts of schizophrenia seem to imply that it is possible to distinguish in a straightforward way human understanding of human problems from, on the other hand, human problems for which scientific explanations must be sought as they are mental illnesses. In other words, the concept of schizophrenia depends on accepting that some things can be understood and other things cannot, although one cannot quantify and objectify them statistically.

But what does it mean to say one cannot understand somebody else? Can human views about the world and other people come from nothing which is meaningful? To answer this question we have to study in detail our patient's life history in order to achieve in the end something of a person's biography. After all, investigating in the realm of psychiatry is frequently more like trying to find the meaning of a poem (or any other kind of text) than researching for the discovery of causes (in physics or chemistry). Further, we must not forget that the concept of cause is now regarded as much more problematic than was the case some decades ago before the appearance of men like Heisenberg (1962) and Bohr (1976).[1]

We will never explain or understand completely another person's life; we can only glimpse at other people's motives and experiences. After all, the same can be said regarding the research activities and achievements of natural scientists. Newton himself could not help confessing:

> I do not know what I may appear to the world, but to myself I seem to have been only like a boy playing on the sea-shore and diverting myself in now and then finding a smoother pebble or a prettier shell than ordinary, whilst the great ocean of truth lay all undiscovered before me.

We are bound to be biased in our version of schizophrenic patients' biographies. Napoleon was not very far from the truth when he said: 'History

1. For a detailed discussion of the problems connected with the distinction between 'reasons' and 'causes' see chaspter 3 of this book.

is only a fable agreed upon'. Nevertheless, this idiographic approach will always be more likely to produce a vivid and insightful picture of patients' past and present behaviour than the official and recommended ways of preparing 'case histories'.

In fact if psychiatrists do not believe in the possibility of understanding what a particular patient says or does they will simply try to gather what they see in advance as the relevant symptoms (in terms of the main nosological entities defined by the diagnostic code with which they agree). They will confirm their own prophecies. The partition of other human beings' subjective reality with the aim of getting a clearer picture of their experiences and flow of consciousness looks like an attempt to obtain a series of mental photographs that would lead us to an easier clinical diagnosis. Attractive and scientific as this may seem, we think this kind of strategy presents the risk of a petrification of patients' mental contents for the sake of a pretentious objectivity and neutrality. By using labels for naming the things we are supposed to be studying we become convinced that we have discovered them, and in a sense taken possession of them, when in the end we were only tilting at windmills and losing opportunities for a meaningful dialogue with our patients. It would actually be very surprising if the doctor could understand his patients using this approach. Having these issues in mind we will be pleading for an imaginative and true-to-life style of clinical history-taking and for a higher degree of awareness of the categorisation we inflict onto patients and our motives for doing so. The danger—and perhaps the aim—of a too forceful and artificial analysis of patients' mental contents, as if we were piling up a number of snapshots, is the neutralisation of the patient as a living individual and his transformation into an object completely distinct in nature, qualities, basic fears and motives from the scientific observer. By this kind of operation the doctor would be implicitly and forever placed in a kind of safety zone from which he could make diagnoses and take decisions protected by his code of label-definitions, that is by his professional discourse. In the words of Michel Foucault (Scheridan 1980):

> Discourse arises when the human capacity of speech becomes highly developed, formalized, submitted to rules, and unfolded under the aegis of a normative concept such as 'the permitted versus the prohibited', 'the rational versus the irrational', or 'the true versus the false'. But the limit on what can be said, and *a fortiori* what can be seen and thought, is set by the 'error' which resides at the heart of any verbal representation of the 'real'.

The attempt to understand our patients' behaviour (and the idiographic approach it presupposes) implies that we are willing to engage in discussion at the patient's level, taking him seriously as a person trying to communicate something (Bateson 1978), or else—in one sense the same thing—as trying to avoid doing so. We must not forget that many views of normal men, although mistaken, are understandable and can *sometimes* be altered by human discussion. Through this discussion we will try to offer to the patient (as honestly as we can) our own ideas and also our opinions about his ideas, but necessarily in a friendly and accepting atmosphere. We hope this exchange of world-views (and the demonstration of our understanding and concern) will eventually lead to a kind of negotiation between us and the patient and even perhaps to a more or less profound and lasting modification of patients' beliefs and lifestyle.

We deliberately chose this kind of approach because it emphasises the similarities rather than the differences between ideas and preoccupations pertaining to human beings ('ours' and 'theirs'). We do not, of course, want to draw any forced and naive parallels between the psychiatrist and patient with regard to their attitudes in the world (*Dasein*). Their situations are different in terms of desirability, and even though schizophrenic patients have a lot to offer and reveal, as far as the nature of the struggles inherent to human life is concerned, their state is one of suffering and perplexity and should not be accepted as a model of mental enlightenment. We disagree with anti-psychiatrists when they say that psychotic patients should be viewed as heroes, more lucid and sane than the average man and engaged in a purifying process of self-cure, a kind of voyage into inner space whose aim is to overcome our normal state of appalling alienation. As Paul Mascari (1979: 336) puts it,

> To explore the patient's metaphors (and most assuredly every clinician, for moral and therapeutic reasons, should attempt to do so) does not imply accepting them. In a sense the world of the schizophrenic is not a possible candidate for endorsement—it is not an acceptable running mate for the better qualified incumbent.

Psychiatrists (still very much under Jaspers's influence) dismiss though too quickly the possibility of understanding these people because their views are unacceptable, and hence they choose from the outset to emphasise the distance that separates us from them. From this irreducible distance they conclude the absolute impossibility of understanding psychotic symptoms and from that they confirm the organic origin of schizophrenic illness.

These ideas are probably derived from what are still considered the objective and scientific ways of approaching and studying reality. If schizophrenics are such a strange and different people they must necessarily belong to another reality, one which has to be dealt with cautiously and detachedly through scientific and objective methods of enquiry. Such a reality cannot be known and understood by means of human involvement and dialogue but only explained by some natural causes.

Obviously there are strong emotional (and political) reasons for accepting this type of explanation without thinking seriously about other alternatives. Approached as objects of scientific enquiry patients could be inspected in a detached and impersonal way, the only correct one for an objective study of their signs and symptoms. This good scientific psychiatrist would therefore be able to collect and evaluate his clinical material in a neutral manner without any preconceived ideas regarding the object he is observing. This model, borrowed from the exact sciences, would imply psychiatrists' potential capacity to eliminate any sources of doubt and perplexity as regards the definition of patients' mental states and to analyse them in terms of their constituent psychological items as an anatomical piece or a microscopic preparation. This model was eventually discarded *even* by the exact sciences; now every physicist knows that the observer is always part of the observed phenomena and cannot adopt towards them a completely neutral and detached posture (Capra 1976).

Although we understand its attractiveness, this is for us an inadequate view of the nature of human interactions. Like the mythical Medusa who changed all the people who dared to look at her into stone, the language of psychopathology can also fossilise the patient, and (the other side of the same coin) the psychiatrist who did not dare to look at his patients' real discourse preferring instead to stick to his code of label definitions. We are not denying the usefulness of psychiatrists' attempts to obtain for themselves a mental construct of their patients' subjective states, as clearly as it is reasonably possible. We think, however, that one should also always stress the political, cultural and historical connotations of professional rituals, and how they can influence the ways we choose to depict our patients' predicament (Stoffels 1975).

'Schizophrenics' Clinical History' Presented as an Example of 'Biography'

One of the main aims of this chapter is to emphasise the need for an idiographic approach to our schizophrenic patients' psychopathology and behaviour. The problem we are considering here by means of this approach is basically: can we learn from these 'disturbed' persons something more about 'what it is to be human'? (as Kierkegaard [1941] insistently asked us to remember). As human beings we are bound to classify the world in which we live in order to find a way among the multitude of facts impinging upon our senses. Nevertheless the nature of this search for the nomothetic relationships connecting the individual cases (that is for the general laws of human behaviour) is inevitably shaped by the particular strategy we have followed beforehand in our operations of data-gathering. The revolutionary work of Levi-Strauss (1966) in the field of anthropology is, in our opinion, a very good example of how a radical change of theoretical perspective can lead to new ways of data-gathering and consequently to the discovery of relationships and similarities previously unsuspected. We are pleading for a strategy of data-gathering that implies approaching our patients' clinical histories as the historian and the novelist approach their characters' biographies. As Christian Scharfetter (1980) puts it:

> The subject matter of psychiatry is always a human being in toto, in the context of his life story. We can get to know this subject matter only if we take the patient seriously and proceed with care towards an understanding of his condition. When we approach in this way those whose lives have gone badly, a psychiatric examination is not a degradation ceremony. The choice of syntax and vocabulary does not then become a negative political act (Laing 1967). We have, after all, long been aware of Nietzsche's seductive power of language...The patient does not have symptoms. He undergoes certain experiences and therefore behaves in a way that deviates depictably from the norm of his group. Nothing in his behaviour can be written off simply as nonsensical. This is not a scientific statement but an acknowledgement of psychopathology as the study of experience and as a signpost to treatment. It embodies the attitude that alone enables us to deal justly with our patients.

In our opinion, psychiatrists tend to use too narrow and naive concepts of understanding and clinical history, mainly in the case of patients diagnosed as psychotic or schizophrenic. We can find here again the influence of Jaspers and *General Psychopathology* where the German author asserts that understanding is only possible and genuine when it happens in a spontaneous, immediate and intuitive way. Writing about Jaspers's concept of understanding, Fish (1966: 270) says:

> Jaspers (1962) suggested that a schizophrenic symptom is one with which the examiner cannot empathise. This means that when the psychiatrist meets a patient with a non-organic mental disorder he tries to put himself in the patient's total life situation and understand the patient's symptoms as a result of his personality, affective state and situational difficulties. If a symptom cannot be understood in this way then it is schizophrenic. This is, of course, a very subjective approach and some psychiatrists are prepared to understand more than others. There are two points which must be stressed. The first is that one must remember that there is a very wide range of human eccentricity, which is not psychotic. The second point is that by empathy or understanding is meant the simple, naive approach and not interpretation in terms of some dynamic psychology.

What does Fish mean by 'simple, naive approach'? When we try to understand what normal people say or do, are we more successful and perceptive in our interpretations by being simple and naive? We are much more inclined to think that our daily attempts to understand other human beings are bound to be problematic, inaccurate and incomplete. The attempt to understand someone's actions and biography is bound to be a complex and painstaking process, necessarily involving an element of deliberate research and the establishment of hypotheses and guesses to be tested in the future. Men and women are by nature difficult to understand even if they happen to belong to the fortunate category of 'normal' people.

Actually to ignore the contribution of human sciences, insights and methods to a more comprehensive knowledge of men's social behaviour and interpersonal relationships would very much hinder the progress of psychiatric theory and practice. Ingleby (1981) wrote:

> The 'decoding' of most symptoms calls for a rather different kind of methodology, which goes beyond the limits of common sense... What is required is a way of accounting for experience and behaviour in terms of meanings, but not necessarily ones which are consciously appreciated either by the agent or his fellows, and this requires a radical revision of both of our conception of the person and of the methods of the human sciences. What has to be replaced is not only the positivist myth of man as machine, but also what Marcuse calls the 'myth of autonomous man' to which interpretative theorists are equally prone. In the place of the unity of the self which is assumed both by phenomenology and common sense, we must substitute Freud's concept of man as fragmented, self-contradictory and alienated from his own experience. Only when this is done can the true meaningfulness of 'mad' behaviour become apparent—and, at the same time, the true madness of ***behaviour which common sense takes to be 'sane'.***

It is interesting to notice that it was Herder (1978), a philosopher and historian (not a doctor or psychiatrist), who first used the word empathy (*Einfuhlung*), meaning by it the ability to imagine and understand past historical events and, through them, value systems and world-views followed by different people and cultures. Psychiatry in fact borrowed this concept from the 'humanities' but since then has handled it in a very parochial, uninspired and meaningless way. Writing about their patients' personalities and mental disturbances psychiatrists have been influenced by the hypothetically timeless and culture-free principles of the so-called psychopathological science forgetting that human behaviour is, most of the time, nothing but a game people play in a particular (and ever changing) historical and social context.

This was also the kind of message put forward by Dilthey (1959), the nineteenth-century German philosopher who was eventually to influence greatly Jaspers's ideas regarding such fundamental concepts in psychiatry's recent history of understanding, personality development and psychotic process. (This is so despite Jaspers's own claim to have been influenced less by Dilthey than by his close friend, Max Weber.) Opposing the tendency prevailing among contemporary human and social scientists to emulate the methodologies and goals of the so-called exact sciences, Dilthey tried to establish the humanities as interpretative (hermeneutic) sciences in their own right (Rickman 1967). This kind of interpretative science would also include psychology, as Roback (1956) stressed when he wrote:

> Both descriptive linguistics and physicalism (which include all stages and grades of behaviourism) are fine in their restricted compass but life deals predominantly with desires and thoughts and feelings, purposes and motives and ideas. If these are to be watered down to stimuli and responses, then our search for the facts is doomed at the very outset. We cannot make a purpose out of a reaction to a sound or a light...any more than we can make a cube out of a square or a square out of a line.

Men could only be properly understood on the basis of a knowledge of all their history; this understanding however could never be final or complete because history itself never is. He wrote: 'The prototype man disintegrates during the process of history' (1956: 6).

Dilthey also emphasised the value of biography as a means of improving our knowledge not only about a particular person's life-productions (or expressions) but also his contemporary society's prevalent world-views. He stressed the element of (more or less deliberate) construction and self-involvement inherently present in the writing of other human being's life-history or biography. Dilthey spent over ten years writing the biography of Schleiermacher, a famous German theologian. Even if a patient's life-history does not usually require such a large amount of time and research from the consultant psychiatrist, we should not nevertheless underrate its enigmas and lightly assume the possibility (or impossibility) of understanding.

These are important issues deserving our attention as psychiatrists: in fact construction and self-involvement are features particularly salient in the psychiatric encounter, a form of dialogue during which both patient (the protagonist) and doctor (the observer) are bound to be involved in the construction of a meaningful life-history, putting their cards on the table in terms of personal values and world-views, even if they very often think they are not doing so.

Dilthey (1959) advocated a 'broad theoretical framework for the objective study of man' and repeatedly called our attention to the role of researchers' imagination and creativity in the study of our socio-historical reality. If we decide to approach schizophrenic patients' personal worlds having also in mind their broad historical and social context, we will be less prone to label their behaviour and experiences as incomprehensible and completely alien to normal human nature.

As Rickman (1967: 37) wrote:

> Understanding as a distinctive approach to human beings is necessary because the human world is pervaded by meaning in a way in which the physical world is not. This does not mean that there is a master plan or overall design in human life, but merely that human actions are accompanied by consciousness and prompted by purposes. They spring from the interpretation of situations and the appreciation of values...The task of the historian, sociologist, social anthropologist or psychologist does not end when he has described this behaviour; he can also discover its meaning by the process of understanding. Ultimately this is based on the fact that we ourselves experience *how* feelings and thoughts give rise to actions.

Knowledge of our historical past (as well as knowledge of a patient's biography) is more like knowledge we claim to have of a friend, of his character, of his ways of thought and action, of the subtle nuances of his personality (so well described by Montaigne [1978] for instance).

'To do this' writes Berlin (1979)

> we must possess imaginative power of a high degree, such as artists, and in particular novelists, require. And even this will not get us far in grasping ways of life too remote from us and unlike our own. Yet even then we need not totally despair for what we are seeking to understand is men—human beings endowed, as we are, with minds and purposes and inner lives. Their works cannot be wholly unintelligible, to us, unlike the impenetrable content of non-human nature. Without this power of 'entering into' minds and situations the past will remain a dead collection of objects in a museum.

This sort of knowledge, not thought of in Descartes' philosophy, is based on the fact that we do know what men are, what is action, what it is to have intentions, motives, to seek to understand and interpret, in order to make oneself at home in the human world: what Hegel (Mazlisch 1966) called *bei sich selbst seien* (to arrive at being at one with oneself).

Is it not surprising that psychiatrists should have bent all their energies to the search for schizophrenia's natural causes, dismissing from the outset all the attempts to understand this particular way of 'being-in-the world', that 'civil world which, since men had made it, men could come to know'? (Vico 1970).

Chapter 3

The Psychiatrists' Praxis, the Language Code of Psychiatry and the Concept of Causality

PSYCHE-TYPE (PSYCHOTYPE)
Then the whole world is all symbol and magic?
It probably is...
And why shouldn't it be?

Álvaro de Campos*

* One of the heteronyms of Fernando Pessoa

IT IS not difficult to understand why psychiatrists do not feel inclined to use their own human potential in their daily clinical tasks. To use our human potential for understanding and concern is to expose ourselves to other people's judgment as well as to recognise that in the end we have no clear-cut and rapid solutions to offer to the patient other than our own assets and insufficiencies as human beings.

This is perhaps the reason why psychiatrists use (and abuse) their jargon, a kind of linguistic cover under which professionals can hide themselves from a confrontation with their patients' problems and predicament. We are not advocating voluntarist and naive solutions for psychiatry's practical problems or denying the need for sophistication in handling our professional duties. Psychiatry is above all a political science (in the Aristotelian sense of the word) concerned with the 'praxis' of interpersonal relationships and finding answers (partial and incomplete as they may be) to the ultimate question: how should men live? We must recognise that psychiatrists' daily tasks (and what they see as their professional duties) are nothing but the result of a political struggle involving professional bodies and institutions over a long period of time. The limits of psychiatry's territory were defined—like the borders of a country—and we are entitled to envisage them being altered in the future (see Goethe). Psychiatry needs a technique, but one upon which we must reflect continuously in order to adapt our guesses and decisions to the test of clinical practice. As Georgin (1981: 8) put it:

> The nosology and semiology which is linked to organic concepts can impose itself on the elements which constitute the body of psychiatric thought. They impose themselves at three levels of discourse on written descriptions, on theorising and on communication. These are not sufficient although they are necessary to produce a science. The nosology, however, presents a real danger, that of inducing a reifying, objectifying discourse from which the subject who speaks is eliminated. It is perhaps necessary to specify the risk in order to see the defensive utilization of nosology in discourse which obscures. To stick to a medical discourse one loses from view the real object by an intricate elaboration within a structure. This then poses the problem of a heterogeneous discourse by the bursting asunder of the medical from the analytical. There is then a turning of an amalgam into articulated and separated discourses and the problem of the integrated relationship between what system speaks and who speaks.

Having said this we wonder how many of the technicalities displayed by psychiatrists' linguistic code derive from a genuine desire to clarify obscure matters and how many are the result of a power game played for the sake of ensuring psychiatrists' status and privileges (Laing 1978). As Kennedy (1980) stressed in relation to general medicine, we think that psychiatrists are tempted to transform human ills into illnesses and, through this linguistic operation, secure the unchallenged power of deciding over such fundamental issues as the life and destiny of huge numbers of people.

Kubie (1971: 308) made this point very clearly when he wrote:

> When such a patient occasionally erupts into open and blind rebellion, I know that it will be called a 'catatonic excitement'. Or, if he consistently covers up his inner turmoil and pain with a 'silly' smile, a giggle, or irrelevant childlike words or gestures, he will surely be called 'hebephrenic'. Of course, these terms have some pragmatic value as a descriptive verbal shorthand, but they are not diagnoses and when such a patient emerges from this state as they do from time to time (if only temporarily) he may surprise us by talking freely and clearly about himself and his seemingly bizarre external behaviour and inner experiences. When this happens we will find ourselves wondering why anyone should ever have expected him to be anything but mute or motionless. From the patient's point of view, was there anything worth saying or doing? Anything that he could have achieved by speaking or acting?

Although accepting that one can hardly speak without using a vernacular, it is necessary to stress that we are also only too aware that the defence of this assumption can very easily degenerate into a rigid and meaningless scientism, the ideology or confidence that modern psychiatry is almost precisely correct in its questions and terminology. May psychiatry be 'trapped in the cage of (its own) language?' (to paraphrase Wittgenstein 1976).

A researcher in the field of schizophrenia has written that 'the broader, less specific and less reliable the criteria used to diagnose schizophrenia, the more likely it is that psychiatrists will be influenced by social and even political pressures and ideologies, and will expose themselves to legitimate criticism' (Wing 1978a: 103). That writer failed to notice that a clear definition of such a controversial entity such as schizophrenia is substantially (at least for the time being) a political decision which means falling in with the power group in psychiatry determining the definition.

We must not forget that for Wittgenstein,

> philosophy should untie the knots in our thinking which we have foolishly put there; but to do that it must make movements which are just as complicated as those knots. Although the result of philosophy is simple, its method cannot be if it is to arrive at that result. The complexity of philosophy is not in its subject matter but in our knotted understanding (Kenny 1976: 52).

Should we (as psychiatrists) not be more aware of the knots in our own understanding and language (not to speak of those knots in our patients' thinking)?

Schneider (1955) himself has always regarded his famous concept of schizophrenia as nothing more than a conventional linguistic device which should be handled as such by the cautious clinician. Huber, Gross and Schüttler (1975: 64) made this point very explicitly when they wrote: 'We can only remember together with Schneider that each concept of schizophrenia represents a convention and that there are up to now very different conventions of what is named schizophrenia'. Nevertheless, a little further in this same paper, Huber *et al.* (1975: 66) cannot help saying that:

> In our opinion the assumption of a disease which is genetically and somatically founded, partly also determined by environmental conditions, and especially the hypothesis of a genetic cerebral enzyme defect acting by neurobiochemical mechanisms, which are susceptible to non-specific stress of all kinds, it is quite compatible with the results of the Bonn study and with all other findings known up to now in schizophrenia.

In our opinion Huber *et al.* have no right to make this kind of assumption regarding the true nature of schizophrenia. Their statements show very clearly how powerful technical language is and how dangerously we manipulate words in order to settle questions that in reality are still waiting for a proper solution. We must not forget that there are choices to be made with regard to the kind of language to use in all those areas of knowledge where clear facts are not overwhelmingly established. These choices create what we take to be real knowledge, and so they imply a certain way of building our own world, even when we are not aware of this fact—we live in the house we have built for ourselves. To ignore the negative consequences brought about by this kind of word-fetishism is particularly harmful when we strive to grasp the richness and variety of our patients' mental life.

When the roads we are not entitled to travel are not yet defined, as is so often the case with psychiatry's theories and techniques, we have to be aware of the problematic nature of the words we have chosen to characterise reality; very often we believe in the absolute value of our own choices and this attitude can make us blind to other possibilities and to other roads to travel.

Psychiatrists' Language Code and the Concept of Causality

Here we would like to exemplify how psychiatrists' professional terminology (that is the words they choose to describe patients' behaviour and experiences) has decisively influenced their prevailing concepts of causality as far as psychiatric illness (in particular schizophrenia) is concerned. The Sapir-Whorf (Whorf 1964) hypothesis, well known in the field of anthropological linguistics, postulates:

> The 'real world' is to a large extent unconsciously built upon the language habits of the group. No two languages are ever sufficiently similar to be considered as representing the same social reality. The worlds in which different societies live are distinct worlds, not merely the same world with different labels attached.

It is, therefore, reasonable to argue that an individual's language may similarly determine his concepts of ill-health. We can actually find relationships between linguistic features and concepts of disease in cultures and societies as varied as the Chinese, Eskimo, Navaho and European. In European languages, for example, it has been suggested that the extensive use of spatial metaphors to express abstract concepts may encourage a more rigid categorisation of disease and inhibit the ability to conceive of multiple factors in disease causation. The use of nouns rather than verbs to express the idea of illness can lead to a static view of disease and tends to separate illnesses as distinct entities rather than defining them as aspects of bodily functioning.

The relationship between man and his environment is complex. In this intricate pattern of transactions we can find a rich reservoir of potential causes waiting to be discovered by means of our diagnostic exercises. Even when we consider the practice of somatic medicine and its scientific endeavours, we arrive at the conclusion that what often is taken for granted as a definitive aetiological theory is nothing more than a way of approaching the world, standing among other ways equally (or even better) suited for our particular purpose. As Wagner (1976: 65-66) wrote:

> The alternate forms, 'he has no illness', and 'he suffers from an illness', imply a definite separation between the patient and his illness. Nowhere in these constructions does one gain the impression of a change of the processes occurring in the individual. Rather a separate entity, illness is added to, or inflicted upon, the individual. There is no implication that he or his processes have any role in the development of the disease. To convey that idea the illness would need to be expressed in verb form (he hypertenses, for instance). I suggested that the form of words we use constrain us from readily accepting the idea that the individual, his personality, and his social and environmental processes re factors in the development of his disease... 'Standard average European' language binds us to a 'standard average European' conception of illness. Although we know a disease to consist of multifactorial changes in biological processes, we continue to think of it as a rigidly defined, unchanging, unicausal object, inflicted upon an individual and distinct from him. In other words a 'thing'. Our conception of disease is only a little less concrete than that of the Eskimos who brush and blow illness away.

We feel there are enough reasons to ask for a more sophisticated way of thinking about causality and aetiological theories in the field of medicine (and psychiatry) and to press, as Totman (1979: 44) puts it in *Social Causes of Illness*:

> for a radical change in our mechanistic style of thinking and talking about illness, and for the adoption of a new concept of health and disease which is more encompassing than the one we have come to accept: perhaps one which is closer to that held in some of the primitive societies mentioned.

The research work carried out so far in relation to the epidemiology of infectious diseases, for instance, shows clearly that the views we hold regarding the specific role of medicine and the right kinds of medical intervention are intimately connected with the implicit (or explicit) ways according to which we conceptualise the causal structure of the world.

If we consider medicine a professional and technical activity with almost exclusive curative aims, we will find ourselves very much inclined to regard the causes of diseases as factors acting upon the human body according to a relatively simple and straightforward catenarian process. As Stacey (1979) wrote:

> From sixteenth century origins, doctors developed new ways of seeing beneath the surface of life, and with this new vision, this 'gaze' as Foucault describes it, modern clinical medicine was born. Disease was no longer seen as something descending from above, but as within the organism... From these beginnings, the gaze deepened until we come to the present day when the vision is focused on cells, and microbiology and the laboratory have come to take a dominant place. Thus clinicians, as scientists, rarely think of living relationships on a larger scale than the human body.

It is perhaps because of this prevailing attitude towards health, disease and causality that we tend to see the steady decline in the mean annual death rates for the infectious diseases (for example respiratory tuberculosis) verified in all the industrialised countries of Western Europe as a mere result of the introduction of chemotherapy (1947), forgetting that mortality from tuberculosis fell sharply from the time when it was first recorded (1838) by virtue of the modification of the conditions that had made tuberculosis so formidable (low resistance to the infection derived from malnutrition and exposure to overcrowding).

Hare (1974: 286-88) tries to demonstrate that (as in the case of infectious diseases) the symptoms, course and prognosis of mental disorders (particularly schizophrenia) have also improved over the last seventy years, under the influence of a variety of social, cultural and economic factors. In this respect, Hare wrote:

> If these changes mean that schizophrenia has become a milder disease in this country, then we must wonder why this has happened. The usual explanation is that treatment—and in particular social management—has improved. But when we remember the evidence that diseases have changed in nature and severity for reasons which are not at all obvious, we should consider the possibility that the same may apply in the case of schizophrenia and that medical treatment may have played only a relatively small part. There is still argument whether the improved prognosis of schizophrenia began before or after the introduction of phenothiazine drugs in about 1957, but my own experiences leaves me in no doubt that the improvement came first... Moreover, if schizophrenia has been ameliorating and continues to do so, we may expect that its severer forms will increasingly give place to the milder and broader disorders of the schizophrenic spectrum; and that would mean that the clinical distinction between schizophrenia on the one hand and affective psychosis, neurosis and personality disorder on the other, would become increasingly blurred in the same way as the Kraepelinian distinction between the subtypes of schizophrenia seems to have become blurred in our day...I do want to suggest to you that psychiatric disorders are changing all the time, that we ought to be carefully monitoring these changes, and that we should at least keep in mind the possibility that part of these changes and perhaps a considerable part, are due to secular processes of a sort which have so often been considered as only peripheral to the conventional concerns of medicine.

Even though Hare (1974) calls our attention to interesting issues, we must add in this connection that we do not agree either with his basic paradigm concerning the nature of schizophrenia or with the way he conceptualises his data. We rather subscribe to the criticisms made by Berrios (1981) regarding Hare's view.

From what has been said, we may conclude that the paradigms (and the concomitant descriptive language on which we base our opinions regarding the real causes of health and disease) are bound to influence what we think we have the right to demand from medicine (and, also, from psychiatry) as a science and as a public service. In his book *The Role of Medicine—Dream, Mirage or Nemesis?*, McKeown (1976: 10) remarked that:

> Medical science and services are misdirected and society's investment in health is not well used, because they rest on an erroneous assumption about the basis of human health. It is assumed that the body can be regarded as a machine whose protection from disease and its effects depends primarily on internal intervention. The approach has led to indifference to the external influences and personal behaviour which are the predominant determinants of health. It has also resulted in the relative neglect of the majority of sick people who provide no scope for the internal measures which are at the centre of medical interest.

Obviously, McKeown's views can also be applied to psychiatrists' clinical tasks, namely to their interaction with psychotic and schizophrenic patients. In fact, the image of the body as a machine susceptible to being repaired by an engineering type of intervention can block, if overwhelmingly predominant, the correct and sensible handling of many instances of somatic illness. The case is even more striking when we consider the condition of psychiatric patients, particularly those suffering from what we call functional psychoses. Stacey (1979) wrote: 'The greatest danger for clinical medicine today is that it is locked into a method of looking at health and ill-health which, while successful on some fronts, is quite unsuccessful on others'. We think the case of schizophrenia is interesting because it exemplifies very well the dangerous consequences brought about by this same method of looking at health and ill-health.

What we are here suggesting is the need for a bolder and more imaginative consideration of the concept of causality in medicine (particularly in psychiatry) and of the tasks and problems confronting the inquiring mind in these fields of research. This attitude does not imply a denial of the need for scientific methodologies for the study of mental disorders but is intended to avoid confusing scientific method with scientism (Gauld and Shotter 1977; Giddens 1974; Harre and Secord 1972). As Stacey (1979) put it:

> The new perspective on clinical ways and means I wish to propose is that those involved in clinical medicine should let their scientific imaginations roam more widely. This means they should back not only research based on cells but also research based upon social relationships, seeking alternative models for health maintenance and disease onset.

The negative consequences of a too narrow-minded concept of causality and aetio-pathogeny (as far as medical and psychiatric disorders are concerned) are exemplified by the history of the discovery of the aetiology of rickets. After the study and observation of many children living in Sheffield's urban area (among whom the disease was very common) scientists concluded that rickets were caused by a deficiency of Vitamin D in the child's body, apparently disregarding the important aetiological role played by the conspicuous lack of sunlight to which those children were chronically subjected (though this factor was obvious in so polluted a town as Sheffield was at that time). It is interesting to note that at the time this discovery was made practically all of Sheffield's doctors lived in the less polluted areas.

This classic example shows the pitfalls of a simplistic theory of causality and, at the same time, the desirability of an approach to our object of study (in this case, the children living in Sheffield who suffered from rickets) that follows several and diversified perspectives. Only in this way can we avoid the danger of accepting as a definitive scientific discovery what is, after all, nothing more than an incomplete and therefore misleading presentation of the causality equation. We also see here how the results of our research strategy are closely connected with the measures we come later to regard as the real or correct therapeutic regime (in this case, tablets of Vitamin D or, on the contrary, a healthy pattern of life with plenty of sunlight, good food and exercise). In a way something very similar may have happened in the history of schizophrenia. A considerable proportion of practising psychiatrists still believe that neuroleptic drugs are the real or correct treatment for the schizophrenic illness. Is the importance of pharmacology and medicine not thereby made more important in human knowledge and our universities? Was not more given to those who had and taken from those who had not? Do we risk exonerating the fog as a human environment?

In the case of a disorder like schizophrenia we face an even more complex system of causal interactions, a system that has to be conceptualised having in mind not a Cartesian (or Euclidean) kind of world-view (such as that implied by psychiatrists' usual linguistic code) but, on the contrary, a transactional or organismic model of the world structure, with emphasis on notions like wholeness, organisation and field (or Gestalt).[1]

Curiously enough, this type of world-making resembles views held by a very old civilisation (many centuries before the rise and splendour of the empiricist attitude, with Bacon, Galileo and Newton). In China, to quote Joseph Needham (1956: 297),

> the implication was that the universe itself is a vast organism, with now one and now another component taking the lead—spontaneous and uncreated it is, with all the parts of it co-operating in a mutual service... In such a system causality is reticular and hierarchically fluctuating, not particulate and singly catenarian. By this I mean that the characteristic Chinese conception of 'causality' in the world of nature was something like that which the comparative physiologist has to form when he studies the nerve-net of coelenterates, or what has been called the 'endocrine orchestra' of mammals... Moreover, it is now becoming probable that the higher nervous centres of mammals and man himself constitute a kind of reticular continuum or 'nerve-net' much more flexible in nature than the traditional conception of telephone wires and exchanges visualised... All this is quite a different kind of thought from the simpler particulate or billiard-ball view of causality in which the prior impact of one thing is the sole cause of the motion of another.

1. The term transactional derives from the impact on biology, sociology, political science, etc. of Dewey and Bentley's (1949) insights concerning society's structure and workings, as against the so-called interactional or self-actional viewpoints put forward by other authors (Bertalanffy 1968).

In our opinion, the approach of psychiatrists to the diagnosis and treatment of schizophrenia would probably be more accurate and meaningful if they decided to conceptualise this disorder (and its possible causes) in accordance with this Chinese model. McKeown (1976: 13) addresses himself to a similar question when he writes:

> There is little evidence of success in the past (with the treatment of mental disorders, that is) for with the exception of the form due to an infection (syphilis of the central nervous system), there has been no response to the influences which have brought about the decline of physical (mainly infectious) diseases...The conclusion to be drawn is that the solution, however distant, of a psychiatric problem such as schizophrenia may come not from treatment of the established disorder by biochemical or other methods but, as in the case of most other major diseases which have so far been controlled, by removal of the influences which led to the abnormality. If so, the main emphasis of medical research should be on identifying those influences by observing and reflecting carefully on the history of schizophrenics and their families, by comparing them with non-affected families, and by examining the experience of the disease in different populations. This is, of course, the approach of the epidemiologist, but he will need even more inspiration than in the study of physical illness. In general he should proceed like Christ rather than Gallup, suspecting the answer before starting to look for it and using subsequent research to provide an opportunity for his hunches to be proved wrong.

We would like to add in this connection that, although we regard the views of McKeown (and Stacey) concerning the problem of causality in medicine as worthy of our attention, we do not consider them radical enough to challenge the old paradigm still governing our current ways of thinking about the causes of somatic or mental disorders. After all, simplistic (and supposedly definitive) sociological theories of causality can involve the same mistakes that have been made in biochemical theories they have set out to criticise. Our criticism of the prevailing theories of causality (particularly, so far as schizophrenia is concerned) attempts to go deeper (in line with Goodman's [1978] ideas) and show how theories are bound to be related to our purposes and to the paths we have decided to follow in order to act upon the world and reality.

Probably because we have not reflected carefully enough upon our professional motives (as psychiatrists and researchers) and also upon the linguistic codes we use to depict reality, we approach the problem of schizophrenia's causality in a fragmented, unidimensional and ultimately naive way. Our main objective so far has been the discovery of the cause of schizophrenia, but like the Greek Chimera this cause has managed to evade all our efforts and theories, perhaps because we have used the wrong words to describe our aims and asked the wrong questions as regards the meaning of our patients' symptoms. Probably we have forgotten that there is no single item causing schizophrenia (as well as our own personality) and there are choices to be made on which aspects to concentrate our attention. As Manfred Bleuler (1978: 604) wrote:

> For half a century the principal aim of students of schizophrenia was assured; they sought to discover the single cause of a disease whose symptomatology and course seemed to suggest one single entity. These studies, however, were not successful. They did not lead one step nearer to the discovery of a specific cause of the hypothetical disease entity, schizophrenia. Today we have to ask ourselves why a specific cause of schizophrenia has not been found. The reason may be simple; perhaps none exists! There may be many different pathogenic factors, together responsible for the outbreak of the disease. Just as we cannot explain the development of the healthy personality by considering a single normal influence, we cannot understand the development of schizophrenia by considering a single damaging influence. In either case, we have to deal with an integration of many dispositions and many influences.

Although in many ways perceptive and enlightening, Manfred Bleuler's remarks are still obviously influenced by the old paradigm's terminology; in fact, referring to schizophrenia, he cannot help using words such as disease, symptomatology, course or outbreak.

Reality's structure and workings do not probably follow a Laplacian kind of 'master plan'. Laplace's (1796) 'world-view' was presented very clearly in his famous dictum:

> To an intelligence, which at an instant in time could know the position of all entities in absolute detail, from the heavenly bodies to the smallest atomic particles, nothing would be uncertain. All of past history and of the future would be available to his eyes.

In this thesis, we would like to underline the relationships existing between this mechanistic approach to the ways of knowing about (and acting upon) the world and the *modus operandi* of our psychiatric institutions. We will endeavour to demonstrate how psychiatrists (and other mental health professionals) have been conditioned in their theoretical views and daily clinical practices by their linguistic habits and concomitant ways of perceiving the reality of being a mental patient.

Chapter 4

An Analysis of the Psychopathology of Schizophrenia

Delusions! Hallucinations! But rationality and hallucination are
driven from the same fountain as that from which springs the
verses of Homer and the stone of the Pyramids.
Everything is the same vital energy,
the same vague vibration,
as is giving a name which says nothing.

Teixeira de Pascoaes

I made of myself something I didn't know,
And what I could become, I didn't.
The fancy costume I put on was wrong.
They saw me straight for what I wasn't,
I didn't disabuse them, so I lost myself.
When I tried taking off the mask,
It stuck to my face.
When I pulled it off and looked in the mirror,
I'd grown older.

Álvaro de Campos (1928)

Introduction

IT WOULD be arrogant and outrageous of us to write believing we were adding the final comments to the schizophrenia debate. However, a degree of over-simplification and dogma puts more clearly what we want to bring to the discussion. We do not wish to impede chemical, electrophysiological and genetic studies. We have attempted many ourselves (for example, Jenner *et al.* 1962; Damas Mora *et al.* 1974; Jenner *et al.* 1975; Howlett and Jenner 1978; Vlissides *et al.* 1986; Allen *et al.* 1991).

Our studies led to a realization of how far from impartial much apparent science is. We set out to extend work that had seemed demonstrated, only to discover the original works to have been mistaken.

We studied the pink spot, neuraminic acid, the abnormality of evoked potentials, changes in cyclic adenyl cyclase, aldosterone changes, nitrogen balance changes and, despite apparently conclusive earlier work, we could repeat none of it. We might be mistaken about the more obvious, to us, state of being human, but our axiom is our belief that we all knew much more before we were so educated about being human! We believe that all human thinking is axiomatic, at least in the sense of having usually hidden but clearly strongly held certainties, or core constructs, on which much of the argument is dependent but which are not themselves certainties. Our axiom is perhaps that it is human to be like us, needing significance and love. The way Wittgenstein (1963) put it was that if one wishes to open a door one must hold the hinges still. The severely intellectual Wittgenstein fails to mention emotion but, in adding elsewhere (1953) the obvious if illuminating statement that questioning must stop somewhere, he in fact expresses intellectually the human dilemma in thought which David Hume (see Magee 1987) so aptly illustrated. Hume wrote that when he left his study he had to act and believe because that is what is involved in being human. The beliefs may be mistaken but are needed; we are human beings.

Our contention is that one hinge in psychiatric discourse is a medical view, much developed in the nineteenth century, that physics, chemistry and mathematics are the basic fundamental sciences. This view is bolstered by their obvious successes. Even in the field of schizophrenia research, the efficacy of phenothiazines is real, as is the release of paranoid states by amphetamine abuse, even if mathematical taxonomy is a chimera. To deny all of that would not be wise, it would be stupid. The central question we pose though is what does that explain? Could it be that human beings all have since birth a paranoid urge? Do they need to be seen as wonderful by others and yet want power for themselves? Or perhaps, in a Freudian (1932) sense, are they always involved in complicated fusions of the tension between their aggressive and erotic (in Plato's sense) urges? If neurosis is the price of civilisation (Freud 1929), it is bought by some repression of the wild animal achieved while nurtured, educated and indoctrinated. Perhaps civilisation is a veneer; or almost, as Goethe put it, the polite (in Germany) are always lying.

If it is true that what we call normal is a socially produced drape over what is natural, and there is a tension involved, some degree of calmness is required to maintain adaptation to the socio-historical situation in which we find ourselves. In this respect, Henry Ey (1963) may have had something to contribute in his organo-dynamique explanations, based on Hughling Jackson's (1958) concept of higher centres playing a role in suppressing the more atavistically automatic action of the central nervous system at lower levels. Perhaps sociability is the highest layer. Human judgment is a subtle gift, not at its best when one is ill or the cortex is over-aroused, which it can be for many reasons. Some causes at least are due to fears and frustrations. Perhaps the same happens after prolonged use of phenothiazines and explains the so-called supersensitivity psychoses (Chouinard and Jones 1978), that is a schizophrenia due to withdrawal from neuroleptics and analogous to benzodiazepine or heroin withdrawal. This could be used then as an argument that schizophrenia is due to excess dopaminergic activity. The evidence that antipsychotic drugs act on dopamingergic systems is good. Dopaminergic systems are certainly activated by amphetamines, which do release psychotic states. Such systems and their sensitivities may also be interestingly studied in terms of the impact of altered desoxynucleoribinic acid, the basic chemical of the genes. However, studies are of most value if they improve human existence. The normal may be the repressed natural person, but perhaps the necessary repression is best changed to enlightened acceptance by honestly facing the human predicament. Sometimes we concede we can only help people to do so by chemically tranquillising them. We are all selfish, egotistic human beings yet needing each other and so rules by which to live together. Human beings seem to us wise to see what is possible and rewarding in social contexts and are helped if that is negotiated with them. Unfortunately, it is difficult while using language to help people to see what has been concretised in it and foisted onto them. It is even more difficult to help them see that others with whom they must live cannot see through what in their complacency they too so conveniently believe. This placid acceptance of being human is painfully difficult to achieve for the religiously fervent, the ardent radical, the nationalist, the angry, the hurt, even for the status-conscious professional. We hope we grasp our own game in producing this book, hoping that we are almost fitting in and yet simultaneously improving our image with at least some. When that is possible it is the course of action we usually recommend for people's mental well being. As in business, there is advantage in mutual vested interest.

We cannot but note, however, that even a work like this produced without fairly secure positions could be dangerous. The by-ways of the academic world are often more tortuous than candid or logical, they too are inevitably human. But we hope that in the same way as the failures of the Christian church can hardly obscure the intentions of the New Testament, the deviations and special pleadings of professionals and academics cannot totally obliterate the intentions behind the concepts of a university to put everything on the table, not least the games being played. As human institutions, like human beings they live and must live with overt or covert tensions. Pure thought or pure science is almost pure fiction. As Goethe put it: 'I can promise to be sincere, but not impartial'.

The viewing of schizophrenia as closer to a life process than to an illness, to use Ciompi's (1980) words, has also important implications in regard to the way we interpret our schizophrenic patients' psychopathology. This issue is a really basic once since a schizophrenic's bizarre and incomprehensible symptoms have often been presented as an argument in favour of the organic or biochemical nature of their disease as well as of the unreasonableness of the attempts to grasp the meaning of what these people say or do. We feel that 'music starts when words fail' and that 'music sounds the way moods feel', and we can understand it.

Nevertheless, we must point out that even clinicians belonging to what is called the classical psychiatric tradition have attempted to understand schizophrenia's psychopathology by means of a more dynamic kind of conceptual model, similar in a way to the models that have been proposed as explanations for the so-called ('understandable') neurotic states.

It is also worthwhile to emphasise (with regard to schizophrenia's psychopathology) that nobody has so far been able to demonstrate beyond reasonable doubt the existence of specific schizophrenic symptoms. Commenting on this, Fish (1966: 270) could not help recognising that:

> It might be thought that Schneider's first-rank symptoms made the diagnosis of schizophrenia very easy, but in fact there are some difficulties. Thus, if the patient is very anxious and perplexed, it may be difficult to be sure whether he really has a first-rank symptom or it is as if he had one.

Is it possible to make such a distinction? Even the popular and widely accepted Schneider's first-rank symptoms (FRSs) have been quite often found in patients suffering from other functional psychoses, and therefore they are far from being pathognomonic symptoms of schizophrenia (Abrams and Taylor 1982; Carpenter, Strauss and Muleh 1973; Silverstone and Harrow 1981). Schneider himself accepted the diagnosis of schizophrenia in the absence of any first-rank symptoms (providing the patient presented the right combination of secondary symptoms, which proves that matters are much more problematic than we feel sometimes inclined to imagine).

Considering now the psychopathological symptoms most frequently searched for by clinicians when they address themselves to the task of diagnosing schizophrenia, we would like to make some comments about these symptoms' official definition and put forward some of the reasons why we do not feel inclined to agree with the definitions.

Schizophrenic Delusions

Schizophrenic delusions are said to be false beliefs coming out of the blue, absolutely unamenable to reason and inexplicable in terms of schizophrenic patients' social and cultural milieu (Hamilton 1985). But how many human mistaken views are really like that? Which circumstances make them more or less so? Are the habitual allegiances, desires, projects and fears of normal human beings logical and rational? What proportion of our normal ideas and beliefs is actually amenable to reason and accordingly modified or abandoned with equanimity?. Is it really so easy and straightforward to explain (or influence) the normal contents of our healthy minds?

Normal people do believe all sorts of strange things (patriotism, religions, ideologies, social conventions, myths) but nevertheless we strive to understand these ideas in terms of childhoods, families, marriages, jobs, careers, countries of origin. Historians also struggle hard to understand famous men's actions, past events, cultures, societies, human ideas and ambitions. Can we learn from their studies and methodology to grasp more sensibly the meaning of schizophrenic patients' psychopathology?

As noted in the previous chapter, Dulthey's emphasis on understanding led psychiatrists (mainly on account of Jaspers's work) paradoxically to envisage (and try to define) what 'could not be understood'. In the process of striving to prove to ourselves our own normality we have (perhaps unwittingly) forgotten what it really means to be human. By doing so we have relinquished too lightly any possible attempts to understand schizophrenics' beliefs, influenced as we probably were by the belief that it would be foolish to try. There has been a tendency, for instance, to diagnose schizophrenics' undesirable beliefs as primary (or autochthonous) delusions although one wonders whether the main practical value of knowing about autochthonous delusions (or any other similar technicalities for that matter) is for passing professional examinations to be psychiatrists.

The experience of human interaction shows, however, that many mistaken ideas called delusions are often quite understandable. In this respect, Freeman (1981) wrote:

> Jaspers' (1963) concept of delusions proper is founded on the fact that patients suffering from schizophrenic and paranoiac psychoses experience these mental events as ego alien and completely unlike previous modes of thinking, feeling and perceiving. This disruption in the continuity and quality of mental life has been taken to indicate that, in contrast to delusion-like ideas, delusions proper do not have psychological antecedents. Such a view has never been acceptable to psychiatrists who favour a developmental approach to mental pathology. According to Minkowski (1927), Katan (1954) and Ey (1969), whose writings are based on Jackson (1894), Freud (1911) and Ribot (1920), it is possible to understand and resolve this disturbance in the continuity of the content of the mental life of those who succumb to schizophrenic and paranoiac psychoses.

We suspect that many so-called delusions are amenable to negotiation within the framework of a trusting interpersonal relationship. Of course, we are only too aware of the strength of patients' commitment to their own world-views and of what these views represent in terms of patients' attitudes to life and other people. It is usually accepted that we can understand the content of many delusions but not the 'form' of this kind of symptom. As has been said, we do not find it at all unwarranted to try to understand this extreme (and strange) form of (mis)communication, most probably intimately related to deluded patients' extreme emotional turmoil and personal predicament. Indeed, for most of us, to be complicit with social conventions is convenient and rewarded. We have in fact incorporated much of our outlook to our own advantage (see Jenner 1984).

Beliefs fulfil very important functions regarding patients' and our most vital and basic needs. It is not difficult to see why they and we stick so firmly to them, even when they and we appear to accept (at least temporarily) the logical arguments intended to disprove their validity. We would like to call attention, in this connection, to the German word for superstition, *Aberglaube* (but believing), since we think it suggests very accurately many deluded patients' ambivalent attitude towards their own 'mistaken beliefs' (at a more or less conscious level).

The existence of this apparently deep-seated dilemma between emotional needs and rational ways of thinking is probably enough to explain why to try to understand a patient's mistaken beliefs does not allow one necessarily to persuade him to give up his idiosyncratic ideas. That can even be a very dangerous threat to his precarious mental balance. In a way this happens to any one of us whenever we feel that our personal beliefs and opinions are being challenged by other people and we are in danger of losing face. We cannot go into it here but the philosophy of logic, like that of mathematics, raises considerable questions about the nature of rules. Here we only want to emphasise the central importance of our emotional stability compared to our views.

Having said this, we maintain that the ability to understand schizophrenic patients' delusions results to a great extent from our willingness to accept that it is worth trying to achieve understanding. The hope is reinforced if we perceive that it is not only patients who hold mistaken ideas or jump to false conclusions. We ourselves must do so too, especially when we strive to grasp the meaning of patients' behaviour and thus project our subjective world-views. Paraphrasing Foucault (1961) we must always remember that 'the person who confesses himself supplies the "raw data" but it is the confessor who gives the "correct meaning"'. Indeed, understanding the patient may itself have more to do with rapport and rapprochement than to some views of logic, more to do with understanding a poem than a mathematical equation.

It is intellectually never as reliable as 'scientific explanations' seem to be, but for the matter in hand, another human being, it is probably more relevant and meaningful. Looking closely at men themselves in order to grasp their ideologies (or, in other words, their delusions), is after all like looking in the horse's mouth with the aim of knowing the state of its teeth.

Formal Thought (and Language) Disorder

Another important psychopathological symptom (in officially recognised ways of diagnosing schizophrenia) is the so-called formal thought (and language) disorder. Many papers dealing with schizophrenic behaviour present this particular type of mental disturbance as a valuable indicator of schizophrenia and consider it a discrete and separate entity, standing apart from other aspects of thinking.

Normal human thinking (like normal human history or normal human social interaction) is not, however, a catenarian sequence of strictly predictable events, without any room for a stochastic development, even though this simplistic view of reality is very often implied by psychiatrists' prevailing opinions of the nature of psychotic signs and symptoms, including formal thought disorders.

Singer (1975), writing about 'the stream of human consciousness', asserted:

> It has often been thought that imagination (or fantasy) eventually disappears from adult mental life, surfacing only during night dreams or occasional fantasies... Freud tended to over-emphasise the power of human verbal and analytical capacities once individuals were freed from neurotic conflict. It seems much more likely from recent research that adult thought is often characterised by a complex mixture of concrete imagery and sensory-related experience with verbal-lexical and analytic coding systems. Indeed it is likely that only a very small percentage of thought is truly carried out in the most purely 'propositional' or abstract form and that most of our thinking involves remembrance of conversations, anticipated conversations, or visual images of particular human interaction.

After all, as we can see from Singer's (1975) comments, normal human beings' formal thought processes are not so different from those of psychotic patients. Foucault (1961) speaks about the increase in the reported incidence of nervous diseases during the second half of the eighteenth century. He quotes a contemporary physician who wrote:

> Do not glory in your state, if you are wise and civilized men; an instant suffices to disturb and annihilate that supposed wisdom of which you are so proud; an unexpected event, a sharp and sudden emotion of the soul will abruptly change the most reasonable and intelligent man into a raving idiot.

As we see, even scientists living during the century of 'light and reason' could not totally trust men's 'rationality' and ability to think in a 'logical' way. Rosenberg and Tucker (1979: 1330), commenting upon the great diversity of 'formal disorder of language and thought' usually presented by researchers and clinicians to prove the 'organic' (and 'ununderstandable') nature of 'schizophrenia' wrote:

> Linguists and anthropologists observe that there are implicit semantic baselines in each culture that create norms for speakers of each sex, age, social class, and so on. The schizophrenic, we would hypothesize, creates a sense of disorder in the listener by subtly deviating from these expectations. The listener may then perceive the deviation as being on a structural or syntactic level. In consequence, we see the long list of attributed defects that have been advanced as the key characteristic of the language of schizophrenics: loose association, concreteness, over-inclusiveness, paralogical thinking, etc. The very diversity of these postulated defects is remarkable. Although they may be descriptively accurate, they are not clearly exclusive. The free speech of normal people is also generally disorganised, especially if a person is in a highly anxious or agitated state. It is obvious that loose associations, blocking and gaps in communication all occur in common parlance. Indeed, they represent the rule rather than the exception in everyday spoken language.

For many authors the disorganisation of schizophrenics' speech (and thought) is intimately connected with their (very understandable) state of emotional distress and with the particular kinds of verbal message they often feel compelled to communicate. In another paper, these same authors (Rosenberg and Tucker 1975: 613) wrote:

> If we examine the 'schizophrenic factor' (obtained by factor analysing patients' speech with the help of several 'verbal content' categories), it becomes apparent that the schizophrenic patient—by his very choice of vocabulary—is telling us about his experiential state. That is, he is exhibiting a heightened concern with the 'self' in a context of distress and disorientation...His use of overstatement, as well as time and space references, bespeaks an agitated need to locate the 'self'...He often pursues closeness itself by such primitive means as aggression or fantasies of devouring the therapist as a means of magical incorporation. The patient struggles to find an acceptable level of intimacy, feeling alternately threatened by closeness and fearful of distance...Their condition seems to represent not so much a suspension of (or defect in) 'ego' processes as an attempt by the embattled (and perhaps defective) 'ego' to survive in the face of extreme stress. It may be that they move toward specificity and overstatement to counteract their fear of dissolution and chaos.

Addressing himself again to the questions brought up by the study of formal thought processes (this time from a somewhat different perspective), Singer (1975) wrote:

> A whole series of experiments has now begun to demonstrate the much greater complexity of adult thought when an attempt is made to tap it on its ongoing flow rather than simply examining the product in the form of a response to a question or problem. It seems clear that examination of the stream of thought from this vantage point supports, for one thing, the literary presentations of the flow of thought by writers such as Joyce. In addition, this research makes clear that ongoing thought in normal adults lacks the formal structure and precision that Freud has attributed to it. What emerges from these experiments is evidence of a rapid shifting of attention to external stimuli, evaluation of the stimuli, resort to recall of early memories, anticipation of the immediate or long-term forthcoming events, and occasionally even elaborate fantasies of events of unlikely possibility in the individual's life.[1]

The accounts of famous scientific discoveries attest very vividly to the decisive contribution of human imagination in the often contorted processes

1. See, for example, James Joyce's *Ulysses* (Paris: Shakespeare Company, 1922) particularly the famous last chapter in which we can follow Molly Bloom's stream of consciousness as she lies in bed. This is also displayed in his last (and most controversial) novel *Finnegans Wake* (London: Faber, 1939).

of scientific research we sometimes suppose completely immune to the wild and illogical assaults of our imagination. Singer (1973) wrote again:

> Reports of scientists' own creative activity indicate how often they have hit upon important solutions to very technical problems through the accounts of striking visual or auditory images. Einstein's fantasy of man shooting out into space and in effect looking back at himself when he travels faster than the speed of light; Kekule's image of figures dancing in circles; Kettering's vision of a flower which suggested the possibilities of a particular engine—gasoline mixture—all are instances in which the poetic mode seems to emerge in imagery form prior to its translation into the more rational verbal—sequential abstractions of pure science.

The often unsuspected similarity existing between us (normal people) and them (psychotic patients), as regards formal thought processes (and their more or less marked disorganisation), is also acknowledged (and demonstrated) by Harrow and Quinlan (1977: 13) when they write:

> The results suggest: (1) disordered thinking is not unique to schizophrenia; (2) distinctions between mild and severe levels of thought pathology are important; and (3) disordered thinking is influenced by acute psychopathology and acute upset. Inferential evidence suggests: (4) disordered thinking fits along a continuum with normal thinking; (5) 'thought disorders' are not a discrete, separate entity, standing apart from other aspects of thinking; and (6) older concepts about primary symptoms in schizophrenia need re-examination (cf. Harrow, Harkavy, Bromet *et al.*, 1973).

Catatonic Behaviour

In our opinion the concept of catatonic behaviour is also very much in need of re-examination. Following the work of Kahlbaum (1974) and Kraepelin (1904), catatonic symptoms have been used as the basis for the diagnosis of one of the main subtypes of schizophrenia, and also as an argument in favour of the somatic origin of this mental disease (Mahendra 1973). However, in the case of functional psychoses like schizophrenia, we do think there are still good grounds for attempting a different approach to this kind of symptomatology. In fact it is not at all out of the question to try to understand schizophrenics' catatonic reactions and relate them to patients' biography and life experiences (see, for example, Jenner and Damas Mora 1983). This is supported in a way by the findings of Venables and Wing (1962: 14) who studied the relationship between level of arousal and social withdrawal in schizophrenic patients. In this paper the authors wrote:

> These results indicate a close and consistent relationship in chronic schizophrenic patients between degree of social withdrawal and level of physiological arousal, whether measured centrally or peripherally. The more withdrawn the patient, the higher his arousal. The only exception to this general rule is found among those patients who exhibit marked coherent delusions without any concomitant incoherences of speech... Thus there is an apparently paradoxical situation—the greater the degree of arousal as measured by skin potential or 2-flash threshold, the lower the motivation of the patient as expressed in his behaviour or in his affective responses... This suggests that the apparently withdrawn patient is in fact more affected by his environment than a normal person. Withdrawal from the environment—both social and material —may then be a protective mechanism. Other work suggests that speech may be affected both in its symbolic and in its motor aspects by disturbances in the arousal system...Arousal level in schizophrenics can be influenced by various drugs, in particular the newer phenothiazine derivatives, and by the social organisation of the patient's environment.

If we take into account the Venables and Wing (1962) data, we think we are entitled to say that it is quite reasonable to regard the withdrawn (and even catatonic) varieties of schizophrenic behaviour as understandable. In our opinion, in the case of functional psychoses the symptoms of social withdrawal, autism, emotional anaesthesia or catatonic retardation can all be regarded as varieties of the same basic defensive attitude or posture vis-à-vis a threatening outside world. It is interesting too that Gjessing (1976) saw catatonic excitement and stupor to be similar states. We see them as often the end result of a chain of reactions very much dependent on understandable human emotions and purposes. This kind of behaviour was traditionally regarded as an expression of a disease process undermining the biological foundations of patients' mental life and supposedly dependent on some sort of metabolic dysfunction. However, as Gjessing showed, some can get perfectly well again.

Actually it is not difficult to grasp why a human being, overwhelmed by disturbing personal conflicts and dilemmas, has to resort to such an extreme kind of ego defence mechanism; for the patient, withdrawal, autism (apparent) emotional anaesthesia, and other similar (self-defeating) defensive reactions, are the only barriers he considers safe enough to protect himself from what he sees as too threatening and dangerous a social environment. At other times, instead of protecting themselves by means of withdrawal (or passivity) reactions, patients cannot help discharging their pent-up emotions through what were usually called reactions of catatonic excitement (or other less dramatic forms of acting-out behaviour). This is so compatible with Gjessing's (1976) formulation that stupor and excitement are expressions of the same underlying problem, to him though one produced by nitrogenous toxins (see, however, Jenner and Damas Mora 1983).

It is interesting to point out here the similarities existing between these unusual (and undesirable) protective strategies and the types of human behaviour often observed during situations of natural disaster, for instance reactions of complete immobilisation or extreme and uncontrollable, psychomotor agitation. In the case of the catatonic schizophrenic, however, the threat comes in fact not from the world of natural elements but from inside the patient himself, mainly from the undesirable mental constructs through which he perceives reality and the intentions and qualities of his fellowmen.

This kind of interpretation is also corroborated by Stone and Eldred's (1959: 16) findings. These authors write:

> It seems likely that in these chronic (schizophrenic) patients an imposed increase in frequency and duration of contacts with personnel was accompanied by the development of manifest delusions. This adds weight to the hypothesis that delusions represent restitutive symptoms as a psychotic attempt to deal with the interplay of internal forces and external reality. Unfortunately, this is often interpreted by nurse and doctor alike as a poor result. The patient becomes more agitated. His orderly routines break down. He is more demanding of staff time and attention. There may be even an increase in suicidal risk...It should not surprise us that a patient whose wall of apathy has been breached would revert to his old screen of projections and delusions, in order to cope with the stress of new relationships. We do not consider the increase in delusions to be necessarily a good or bad turn. We do think that it may be an inevitable occurrence in the rehabilitation of certain chronic schizophrenic patients.

Challenged by doctors or nurses (and asked to interact more actively with a fearful outside world), schizophrenic patients (even if they happen to be of the withdrawn and institutionalised type) tend to defend themselves, as we can see, in very extreme ways from what they feel is a dangerous encroachment upon their disturbed private lives and fragile mental balance; perhaps their social behaviour is more understandable in this particular context than we are usually inclined to concede.

Hallucinatory Experiences

Hallucinatory experiences also rank high among the psychopathological symptoms normally used for the diagnosis of schizophrenia. Nevertheless we quite often tend to forget that these bizarre mental experiences are susceptible to very different kinds of approach and cannot be taken for granted as if their definitive explanations had already been found. There are now particularly interesting Dutch studies on the widespread experience of hearing voices (see Romme and Escher 1989). Many people do so and yet live overtly undisturbed lives.

De Clerambault (1974), for instance, who supported a strictly neuropathological explanation for the appearance of schizophrenic hallucinations maintained (very understandably, in view of his own paradigm) that the central stimulation causing the hallucination imposed itself so powerfully on the patient that 'he must be crazy not to believe it'. De Clerambault wrote in this respect:

> The delusional belief (in the 'hallucination', that is) is the reaction of that part of the mind and emotions that is still healthy to be an automatism which arises spontaneously and takes the patient by surprise at a time when he is quite calm both emotionally and mentally.

He saw the schizophrenic patient therefore, not as an emotionally (and socially) disturbed individual who tries to communicate his distress in a particularly unusual and undesirable manner, but on the contrary as a quite healthy and calm human being (at least partially) who happens to be suddenly attacked by strange experiences totally alien to his own will, feelings and world-views.

We must not forget, however, that (already many centuries before De Clerambault) the Greek doctor Asclepiades (a true pioneer in the humane treatment of mental patients) held what is in our opinion a more sophisticated view regarding the nature of hallucinations. In fact he defined hallucination as a representation which has worked its way up to the strength of a perception due to a weakening of the control-apparatus of the mind. His views were to be confirmed much later, for instance by the experimental work of L'Hermitte (1961) and Ajuriaguerra (1954). These authors concluded that a direct stimulation of the central nervous system could never give rise to sensations of the hallucinatory type unless they occurred in the context of a more or less marked disturbance of the patient's whole personality. Their findings also supported what Baillarger (1846) had already observed in relation to the stimulation of the sense-organs themselves; certain sensations could occur this way but never 'true perceptions', unless 'the imagination is disturbed at the same time', to use his own words.

Even though authors like Schneider have not explicitly proposed any specific theories concerning the aetiology of schizophrenia, we think a considerable proportion of practising psychiatrists still believe that Schneiderian auditory hallucinations must perforce derive from some kind of organic (neurophysiological?) process disturbing the workings of the brain. It is worthwhile to stress in this respect that symptoms of a psychotic kind (among them hallucinations) have been quite often observed not only during the course of organic brain syndromes but also in the case of functional psychiatric disorders probably with a psychodynamic explanation (such as, for instance, the Ganser syndrome, which has been classified among the hysterical dissociative states) (Schatzman 1980).

This way of thinking fails to take into account that a given symptom, impressive and strange as it may seem, does not necessarily imply by itself the presence of any definite causal mechanism—the evaluation of this symptom's meaning and significance requires a broader kind of diagnostic approach, one that interprets each individual symptom in the global context of patients' behaviour, personal experiences and physical state.

In his book *Due hashish et de l'alienation mentale* (1845), Moreau de Tours, the French psychiatrist, has also pointed out that the problem of hallucination does not lie in the symptom itself but in the totality of what he called the sick personality. Van den Berg (1982) in this respect wrote:

> Moreau does not intend to determine an organic basis; he wishes to know in modern language of what the *psychological prerequisite* for hallucinations consists. This 'fond mental' or 'cause essentielle' he finds in the 'fait primordiel', which is of a wholly psychical nature and which, according to him, shows itself most clearly in 'versatile excitation'... Moreau de Tours then expresses his view in this almost paradoxical yet lucid aphorism: 'It is not proper to talk of hallucinations but rather of a hallucinatory state'.

A little further in the same paper, Van den Berg wrote:

> A hallucination, like any other artificially isolated phenomenon, can only be rightly observed in a study of the psychical totality, which is disturbed in some way. This being disturbed should be the first and foremost subject of the study...In accordance with the fact that, phenomenologically speaking, hallucinating cannot at all be equated with perceiving, there is however an intimate connection between hallucinating and that special psychical totality which typifies the sick persona. Hugenholtz expresses this as follows: 'Hallucinating has a content, which fits in the psychical totality of the soul'...*It appears expedient to me to emphasise that there is not only harmony between hallucinating and that psychical totality in terms of content, but also in terms of form*...By concentrating on the content one becomes blind to the form in which the patient presents him, or herself, during the time we spend with him. If there is no sensitivity to that form, that is to the way of relating, then we may not expect any such sensitivity in a theory of hallucinations either!

Van den Berg's approach to symptoms like hallucinations is therefore quite different from Schneider's (and also from the approach of all the proponents of those systems and methods of clinical evaluation that have been more or less directly influenced by Schneider's viewpoints—the P.S.E. [Present

State Examination], for example [Dinnage 1980]). In another passage of the same paper, Van den Berg (1982) comments:

> This totality of being and relating, which Moreau de Tours indicated by the term *fait primordiel*, should be the first subject of any phenomenological analysis of the phenomenon of hallucination. This *fait primordiel* cannot be covered by the concept of 'consciousness' though the tendency existed to do just that... It would be better to speak of the disposition of the patient, the way he finds himself, the way he is disposed, or shortly the 'state of mind' of the patient. (This refers to Heidegger's concept of *Befindlichkeit*, often translated as moodedness or state of mind). Man always has *Befindlichkeit* (from *sich befinden*—to find himself or to feel). The term 'disposition' here also includes a historical perspective. For example, Jelgersma in his handbook for psychiatry points explicitly to the harmony which exists between the mood of the patient and his hallucinating. Furthermore, he rightly remarks that the disposition and mood change first—'a psychosis never starts with hallucinations'.

Van den Berg does not seem to accept, therefore, the existence of primary (or out-of-the-blue) schizophrenic symptoms, particularly hallucinations. He calls our attention to the fact that in the person of the schizophrenic patient we are facing a human being disposed (on account of what we think are quite understandable human reasons) to an undesirable style of interpersonal (mis)communication, not just a diseased brain whose twisted molecules cannot but produce twisted thoughts and unreal perceptions.

It was Linus Pauling (1973), twice winner of the Nobel Prize, who said: 'There are no "twisted thoughts" without "twisted molecules"'. We feel very much inclined to think the contrary and his *bon mot* was clever rather than wise: almost all long molecules are twisted.

In a paper written by Horowitz (1975) we can find an analysis of hallucinatory experiences very much in line with Van den Berg's position:

> In hallucinating experiences information is represented in image form rather than in the enactive or lexical modes...Such shifts to a preponderance of image representation can occur because of psychological motivation as well as physiological alteration of substratum. Emergent but warded-off ideas and feelings may gain expression as unbidden images. The translation of these images into word meanings may be impeded as a defensive operation.

For Horowitz (1975) the intrusiveness of these images, due to a gradual intensification of their frequency and vividness, could result in them being erroneously regarded as real perceptions by an emotionally disturbed (or disposed) patient; this author ascribes thus a preponderant role (in the building-up of patients' hallucinatory experiences) to patients' motives, desires and emotions—in his model, the relative intensification of internal sources of information could occur under diverse circumstances, such as 'the augmentation of internal input due to arousal of ideas and feelings secondary to wishes, needs and fear states' (for example, hallucinations of the lost spouse reported by widows or widowers).

The role of schizophrenics' psychodynamic processes (as regards the origin of their hallucinations) is also acknowledged, in the context of a very different kind of approach, by Slade (1973: 296). In a paper dealing with the behaviouristic treatment of schizophrenic hallucinations, Slade puts forward the following conclusions:

> The main focus of interest was the elucidation of psychological mechanisms underlying the experience of auditory hallucinations. In an initial investigatory period evidence was found suggesting that the patient's voices tended to occur when he was in a state of high internal arousal produced by exposure to a variety of social situations. Treatment involving gradual exposure to these situations, while in a relaxed state, led to a lowering of the patient's general arousal level, together with a gradual decrease in the frequency of recorded voices.

Slade shows, therefore, that states of high arousal (and the concomitant schizophrenic psychopathology) can very well be dependent on a variety of meaningful social interactions which are perceived by the patient as especially threatening to his precarious sense of personal security. In Judkins and Slade (1981) 'A Questionnaire Study of Hostility in Persistent Auditory Hallucinations', the authors demonstrate the existence of a significant correlation between the level of schizophrenic patients' hostility feelings and, on the other hand, the duration and intensity of their auditory hallucinations.

A similarly broad-minded approach to schizophrenic hallucinations is presented by Freeman, Cameron and McGhie (1965). Speaking about disturbances in perception (ch. 7), these authors comment:

> Probably the most frequent perceptual disturbances in schizophrenia are auditory hallucinations. In normal psychiatric usage this term describes the condition where the patient 'hears voices' which appear to have their source in the external environment. In a recent article, Karagulla (1955) objects to the common tendency to regard these phenomena in such a narrow way and makes an interesting analysis of the range of such perceptual disturbances. In 'schizophrenia' the patient is continually troubled by ideas which are presented to him independently of his volition. Some appear to him as though emanating from voices in the external environment. These, the commonly accepted auditory hallucinations, represent in our opinion but one gradation of this experience. The term 'auditory hallucinations' cannot be made to cover all the modes of perception of this phenomenon, nor does it sufficiently stress its intricate nature, the intimate relationship which exists between it and the patient's own thought.

> In some patients those alien ideas appear as 'thoughts differing only slightly in quality from the silent imperceptible flow of normal thinking'. This concept of a gradation of hallucinatory experience would seem to be important in our understanding of the fully developed, bizarre type of hallucinations one finds in chronic schizophrenia.

Even though we cannot but disagree with some of Karagulla's ideas he rightly emphasises not only the intimate relationships existing between hallucinations and patients' psychodynamics, but also the similarities connecting these seemingly alien experiences with certain varieties of the normal state of consciousness. However, what does Karagulla mean when he says that 'schizophrenic patients are presented with alien ideas independent of their volitional control'? Is this a mere *façon de parler* or is Karagulla really convinced that patients' thoughts are not their own thoughts? In this connection we agree with Thomas Szasz (1976: 313) when he writes:

> Now, while asleep, psychiatry still dreams about it [G.P.I. that is]; while awake, it sees the world as if the spectre of paresis lurked behind every foolish face or troubled thought. Thus has the image of the crooked spirochete making people mad been replaced in the minds of many psychiatrists by the image of the crooked molecule making them mad.

Horowitz (1975) makes the point that,

> perception is a constructive process governed essentially by two needs: the need for accurate knowledge of reality and the need to find what is hoped or feared may be 'out there'. The latter purpose directs perception and is called 'expectancy', a priming of certain schemata for matching with potential patterns. Suppose there is highly tonic schemata, the result of an intense need state. Because of dual input the internal schemata might be matched with the perceptual nidus and the composite image would yield a perception-like experience. In intense need states no perceptual nidus is necessary. Freud called this process of internal input gaining representation as if it were external input 'topographic regression'. He suggested that such freeing of the inhibitions on internal input might have adaptive purposes...Thus a hallucination may fulfil some aspects of needs, however, temporarily, and these satisfactions would reinforce whatever changes in controls made hallucinations possible in the first place.

In addition to stressing the wish-fulfilling nature of some hallucinatory experiences, Horowitz (1975) also calls our attention to the potential rewards patients can get from their hallucinations and to the concomitant process of reinforcement that can lead to the future repetition of these same kinds of experiences. In this connection, we would like to point out that we are completely dependent on our patients' accounts whenever we have to decide whether they are (or are not) suffering from hallucinations. In fact, on account of the entirely subjective nature of this experience, we find ourselves deprived of any objective criteria for the validation of our patients' statements; we have to accept their words and try to find their real meaning with the help of what we already know about these patients' clinical conditions and biographies.

Commenting on the criteria chosen by the organisers of the 'International Pilot Study of Schizophrenia' (World Health Organisation 1973) as 'standard guidelines' for the 'correct' diagnosis of 'schizophrenia', Szasz (1976) addressed himself to a similar question when he wrote:

> *Hallucinations*—no problem here either; communicating with the deities or dead people (and being unsuccessful at claiming a 'divine calling' or being a spiritualist); or seeing one's childhood or other long-past events (in one's mind's eye) and relating them to someone who insists that the speaker 'actually' sees them.

Of course Szasz's witty comments could be dismissed as irrelevant as they do not refer to the true or typical schizophrenic hallucinations. Nevertheless, even if we do not question the meaning of the words 'true' and 'typical', Szasz's remarks are useful and enlightening in the context of a discussion concerning schizophrenic hallucinations. In fact, what is important in Szasz's comments is his calling our attention to clinicians' insistence on attributing a hallucinatory character to their patients' subjective experiences (or, more precisely, to their own statements about them).

This is a very interesting way of approaching this problem since traditional textbooks of psychiatry regard patients' insistence on stating the reality of their hallucinatory voices as the most decisive criterion for the correct characterisation of this experience, forgetting that what really matters here is the interpretative model doctors feel inclined to use in order to define (and label) their patients' behaviour and speech. Actually, if a schizophrenic repeatedly asserts that he hears voices, the most we can say is that he insists on telling us that he hears voices; from his statements we are not entitled to infer any sort of similarity (let alone identity) between the subjective experiences he reports to us and what we usually call normal perceptions.

Obviously, his undesirable behaviour and ways of speaking show how disturbed he is and how difficult it is for him to communicate with us in a socially acceptable manner; nevertheless, disturbing and undesirable as they may be, hallucinations can very well be regarded as special messages patients use to convey to their fellow human beings their statement of personal distress and emotional turmoil.[1] This is the point made by Dinnage (1980) when, commenting on Schatzman's book *The Story of Ruth* she wrote:

> We also have to consider, apropos of Ruth's trances and impersonations, how normal and deeply rooted is our tendency to dramatize our inner life... We take for granted the extraordinariness of a play or novel that presents us with a whole world of people whom we discuss as if they were real; but the fact that Hamlet did not exist before Shakespeare crystallised a part of himself into the character is really as odd as anything reported here. Writers have reported over and over again that at times their work seems as if 'given' from somewhere else; actors and actresses find themselves inventing a whole human being out of the pages of a script. If our ordinary fantasies could be instantly scripted, acted and transposed to a television screen, they would no doubt be amazing.

It must be remembered that schizophrenic patients cannot be expected to achieve a completely accurate description of their own mental states; like any other human being, they are also conditioned from the outset by the limited possibilities of their own vocabulary and are therefore bound to speak about themselves (and other people) by means of an 'as if' (and necessarily inadequate) kind of language.

Horowitz also refers to this point:

> The strangeness of an initial image may be maintained in the phases of appraisal after the initial image episode, phases that may relate to a memory of the image episode, a memory itself subject to continuous revision. This kind of information processing follows certain rules or plans. One set of rules corresponds to the reality principle, particularly to the differentiation of reality from fantasy. But, as in the example of hallucinating food in order to restore physiological homeostasis or to sustain psychological hope, what is most adaptational may be to discard ordinary rules and accept fabrications as if they were real. In such conditions as states of intense need, the reality principle would be derailed in favour of the pleasure principle. Such derailment would contribute to the acceptance of image experiences as if they were real. Restitutional hallucinations in schizophrenia might be a case in point.

Horowitz accepts, therefore, the intervention of patients' motivational systems not only during the activation of the imagery processes that eventually lead to hallucinations but also in the subsequent phases of evaluation and

1. See in this connection Haley's (1976) research in the field of 'information theory' and its application to the analysis and interpretation of 'schizophrenic' patients' behaviour and speech.

reporting of such experiences, the period, that is, during which patients commit themselves to the difficult task of choosing what they think are the right words to describe their mental states.

In this brief discussion of so-called schizophrenic hallucinations it should be pointed out that hallucinatory experiences of very diverse forms and contents are commonly reported by normal individuals undergoing hypnosis. In fact, these people, by a process of induced (or self-induced) suggestion, are able to experience memories of events and emotions as if they were current realities.

Mellet (1980: 29), for instance, defines hypnosis as an

> unusual (or altered) state of consciousness in which distortions of perception (possibly including those of place and time) occur as uncritical responses of the subject to notions from an objective source (usually the hypnotist) or a subjective source (his own memory) or both.

Hallucinatory experiences do occur in induced (or self-induced) hypnotic states, a fact that apparently proves the existence of a natural disposition in normal human beings to experience (and sometimes produce by themselves) qualitatively different states of consciousness and perceptive disorders. Orne (1973) wrote: 'It is not unusual feats of motor behaviour (such as being able to lie suspended horizontally by the ankles and the back of the neck between two chairs) that are indicative of a hypnotic state. The important entity is distortion of perception.' As Mellet (1980) put it: 'There are many techniques but the hypnotist is always a facilitator of a natural process available to any individual'. For Barber (1969) all hypnotic phenomena derive from a process of role-playing, basically dependent on the hypnotised individual's particular level of motivation. Barber and Wilson (Dinnage 1980) present an identical conceptual model of the nature of hypnotic states and adduce detailed factual evidence that seems to confirm the validity of our attempts to relate schizophrenic hallucinations to hypnotic experiences.

Hypnotic states (the unusual states of consciousness basically characterised by distortions of perception and probably dependent on a more or less conscious motivation to regress to a more primitive level of mental functioning) are in a way also related to other very interesting clinical conditions, the so-called hysterical reactions. Mears (1960), for instance, regarded hypnosis as a state of atavistic regression, a 'return to a more primitive form of mental function in which logical critical thought is suspended and emotion is left uncontrolled'. We refer here to hysteria because we think the study of its varied psychopathology can contribute to a better understanding of schizophrenic behaviour.

We must not forget that these bizarre mental disorders (which the famous Charcot initially attributed to the intervention of organic causes) only became generally accessible to human understanding after Freud had put forward his now well-known insights. If now we find it reasonable to try to understand hysterical patients' motives and conflicts, why should we not be entitled to do the same in relation to schizophrenics' psychopathology? Surely, when a hysterical patient says he is not able to see or hear (even though we know he has perfectly sound eyes and ears), he does not behave less strangely (or undesirably) than a schizophrenic who says he sees or hears something that is not actually out there!

When we read about hysterical hallucinations, it is usually underlined that they are typically visual in nature and so basically different from true schizophrenic hallucinations (characterised by their more or less complex verbal content). Nevertheless, hysterical states are not at all incompatible with patients reporting auditory hallucinations. Wijsenbeck *et al.* (1980), for instance, wrote about a 39-year-old married woman, mother of four children, who was admitted to a psychiatric hospital presenting (among other symptoms) auditory hallucinations. Commenting on these experiences, the authors wrote:

> The auditory hallucinations were stimulated by being in a taxi, a situation concretely associated with her husband's work as a taxi driver (she hallucinated a man's voice which ordered her to jump out every time she took a drive in a taxi...She wondered what it could be and checked behind, but nobody was there). As she was ambivalent towards men—a feeling which had dominated her attitude from childhood—her aggressive drives towards her husband were repressed and substituted by guilt feelings. The taxi hallucination seemed to represent projected aggression toward the object of ambivalence. In this way she could escape her guilt feelings and at the same time express aggression.

According to the authors, this patient's life-history (and understandable motives) were enough to explain her symptoms (including the auditory hallucinations), without being necessary to pinpoint or postulate the intervention of any specific organic factors. They conclude their paper with the following remarks:

> We believe that this type of psychogenesis and phenomenology in a non-psychotic and non-dissociative patient represent hallucinations of conversive origin, and in many ways fit the description of Fitzgerald and Wells (1977). We wonder whether their rarity in the literature represents a small prevalence or merely the fact that these cases do not seek or reach psychiatric help unless other difficulties are involved...Just as conversion blindness or deafness some

> times manifest themselves as blocking perception at one end of the spectrum, we believe that hallucinations represent a more complex expression of conversive symptomatology on the overstimulation side of the spectrum.

In this connection it is worthwhile to point out the very original and insightful study of hallucinatory experiences produced by the French philosopher Merleau-Ponty (1945) in his book *Phenomenology of Perception.* In our opinion, he managed to extend the analysis of human mental states and subjective experiences far beyond the narrow limits usually defined (and imposed) by traditional textbooks of psychiatry. Speaking about hallucinations, for instance, Merleau-Ponty writes:

> Hallucination causes the real to disintegrate before our eyes and puts a quasi-reality in its place, and in both these respects this phenomenon brings us back to the pre-logical bases of our knowledge and confirms what has been said about the thing and the world. The all-important point is that the patients, most of the time, discriminate between their hallucinations and their perceptions...The fact that patients so often say that someone is talking to them by telephone or radio is to be taken precisely as expressing that the morbid world is artificial, and that it lacks something needed to become a 'reality'...All the difficulties arise from the fact that objective thought, the reduction of things as experienced to objects, of subjectivity to the 'cogitatio', leaves no room for the equivocal adherence of the subject to pre-objective phenomena.

Calling our attention to points also referred to by Thomas Szasz (1976) regarding the evaluation (or clinical interpretation) of hallucinatory experiences, Merleau-Ponty (1945) said a little further in the same book:

> When the victim of hallucinations declares that he sees and hears, we must not believe him since he also declares the opposite; what we must do is understand him. We must not be satisfied with the opinions of sane consciousness on the subject of hallucinatory consciousness, and regard ourselves as sole judges of the distinctive significance of the hallucination...*I am sitting before my subject and chatting with him; he is trying to describe to me what he 'sees' and what he 'hears'; it is not a question either of taking him at his word, or of reducing his experiences to mine, or coinciding with him, or sticking to my own point of view, but of making explicit my experience and also his experience as it is conveyed to me in my own, and his hallucinatory belief and my real belief, and to understand one through the other...* Hallucinations are associated with a certain sensory realm only insofar as each sensory field provides the distortion of existence with particular possibilities of expression. The schizophrenic's hallucinations are predominantly auditory and tactile because the world of hearing and touch, in virtue of its natural structure, is better able to stand for an existence which is possessed, jeopardised and deindividualised... The victim of

> hallucinations does not see and hear in the normal sense but makes use of his sensory fields and his natural insertion into a world in order to build up, out of the fragments of this world, an artificial world answering to the total intention of his being.

The hallucinatory experience can, therefore, be regarded as another undesirable consequence of the peculiar way schizophrenic patients build (or perceive) the world standing before their eyes, ears or tactile receptors. Considered in this light, hallucinations are not necessarily the mechanical result of some organic brain disease, as De Clerambault, for example, would like to have it; they can also represent a distorted (and alienated) way of expressing one's human predicament to (more or less receptive and understanding) other people. Merleau-Ponty (1945) commented in this respect:

> The food refused by the victim of hallucination is poisoned only for him, but to this extent it is poisoned irrefutably. The hallucination is not a perception but it has the value of reality, and it alone counts for the victim...However different it is from perception, hallucination must be able to supplant it and exist for the patient in a higher degree than his own perceptions. This can be so only so long as hallucination and perception are modalities of one single primordial function, through which we arrange round about us a setting of definite structure, through which we are enabled to place ourselves at one time fairly and squarely in the world, and at another marginally to it.

Conclusion

In the light of what we have written concerning schizophrenia's psychopathology, we think we are entitled to assert that the nature of schizophrenic patients' symptomatology is not in itself reason enough for us to dismiss as unreasonable and unwarranted an attempt to understand these patients' experiences and behaviour in terms of their biographies. In our opinion, we need arguments stronger and more relevant than the supposedly bizarre schizophrenic symptomatology in order confidently to classify as risible and mistaken what we call the humanistic approach to schizophrenic people and their psychopathology.

On the other hand, we cannot produce any evidence which entitles us to invalidate attempts to study the hypothesis that some so-called schizophrenic symptoms are best explained in terms of some neuropathology of the brain.

Chapter 5

Schizophrenic Behaviour and Social Psychiatry Research

Today I'm torn between the allegiance I owe
To something real outside me—the Tobacco Shop across the street,
And something real inside me—the feeling that it's all a dream.

Álvaro de Campos (1928)

WE THINK the kind of 'paradigm' we are proposing here for the conceptualisation of schizophrenia is also consistent with the empirical results achieved by researchers working in the field of social (or community) psychiatry. At the same time, we do not like the label of social psychiatry; all psychiatric praxis is bound to be social and must take into account the community where patients live their more or less disturbed lives.

For instance, the conclusions reached by Tarrier *et al.* (1979) could have been easily anticipated had we envisaged the schizophrenic patient as a highly sensitive person, living in a more or less permanent state of emotional turmoil, especially when interacting with people he perceives as threatening or dangerous. These authors concluded their paper with the following remarks:

> Psychophysiological measures made on schizophrenic patients in the laboratory fail to detect important differences apparent when the patients are tested in their own homes. The innovative procedure of testing patients at home indicates that the laboratory is an inappropriate setting for measures of schizophrenic patients' reactivity to their social environment. Psychophysiological measures change significantly when schizophrenic patients are exposed to novel situations such as a life event and the atmosphere generated by a high EE (expressed emotion) relative. This supports the unifying concept of arousal used previously to explain the provocation of schizophrenic relapses by these social situations. The sensitivity of psychophysiological measures to the schizophrenic patient's social environment allows us to monitor attempts to change the environment. This deserves high priority for those schizophrenic patients living in a deleterious social environment at high risk of relapse.

Having in view a humanistic approach to schizophrenia, the way chosen by these authors to characterise the multiple interactions between schizophrenic patients and their more or less varied social environment seems probably too simplistic and schematic; nevertheless, provided that we remain aware of the fact that their results can be interpreted at different levels of conceptualisation, we find these authors' research quite useful since, far from contradicting our paradigm, their findings can be fitted in with this approach and used to corroborate it.

This also applies, for instance, to the conclusions reached by Leff *et al.* (1973: 660) in another paper:

> Trials of maintenance phenothiazines carried out on schizophrenics in hospital do not generally show such a marked advantage of active drug over placebo as trials performed on out-patients. This suggests that the hospital environment

> itself has a protective effect in shielding schizophrenics on placebo from many of the stresses they counter when living with their families (Brown *et al.* 1972). Schizophrenic patients living in the community and not taking drugs seem to relapse as a result of the disturbing effect of everyday social interactions. Only patients on maintenance therapy are protected against the stresses implicit in uneventful social intercourse and are unlikely to relapse unless exposed to some additional stress in the form of one or other life event as measured in this study.

In this connection, we can also quote Vaughn and Leff (1979):

> Brown and others have suggested that social withdrawal can be a means of coping with a stressful situation, a protective mechanism which lessens chances of relapse of schizophrenia. Investigation of this possibility revealed a significant association between low face-to-face contact and social withdrawal in patients from high EE homes (exact $P = 0.023$). Within the high EE group, two-thirds of those who were socially withdrawn or avoided family members in the months preceding key admission were well at follow-up, while 58% of those who did not show signs of withdrawal later relapsed. This suggests a general coping style and provides further support for the notion that the person suffering from schizophrenia does exercise some control over the course of his illness.

A little further, these same authors conclude their paper with the following suggestions:

> This brings us to yet another kind of intervention: efforts to change the attitudes of over-involved or highly critical relatives. At the moment we know very little about the formation of such attitudes and their susceptibility to change, which makes this suggestion speculative. But an analysis of the determinants of relatives' expressed emotions would provide clues as to how one might best intervene. For example, in considering how to deal with a highly critical relative, it would be useful to examine systematically the relative's complaints—to carry out, in effect, a content analysis of his responses. Are his remarks directed at long-standing personality traits of the patient, or are they primarily about illness-related behaviours?

Even though we do not agree with the authors' terminology (and their underlying paradigms), it is encouraging to find social psychiatrists willing to listen to what patients (or their relatives) actually say or do. It seems at least some researchers working in this field do not find it necessary to obey the principles of detached observation so strictly as, for instance, Heimowitz and Spohr (1980: 288). In fact, describing the testing procedures they have applied in their research, these authors wrote:

> Testing always began with four standard interview questions to facilitate developing a rapport with the subjects. These included: (a) How have you been feeling? (b) How did you come to be in the hospital? (c) How do you like it here in the hospital? (d) Tell me about some of your problems and about some of the things that bother you.

A little further, speaking about what they call 'the verbal behaviour analysis of psychological defence mechanisms', these authors presented the following items as possible ways of measuring schizophrenic abnormality:

> *Direct references*: all references to the experimenter or experimental method, considered indicative of a maladaptive defensive manoeuvre and loss of an attentional focus; *Evaluation*: use of all value judgements is scored and considered to relate to externalising and, possibly, projective defenses.

We regard this last passage as paradigmatic concerning what we have been attempting to say about the different methodologies that have been used to study schizophrenia. It shows very clearly how far our misguided attempts to achieve objectivity can damage the meaningfulness (and ultimate efficacy) of doctor-patient relationships. The need for a more meaningful and sensible (although apparently less objective) analysis of schizophrenics' psychopathology was very well stressed by Korer (1980):

> The phenomenological method can, if used without thought and insight lead to an approach to schizophrenia which is on the highest level of generalisation—the common, formal elements of external 'symptom-spotting' being deemed sufficient to make the most routine of diagnoses. This may be adequate when making a diagnosis for a pharmacological treatment regime and it is certainly useful in its role as a research instrument when many numbers of potential subjects need to be seen and standardisation is necessary to ensure consistency and reliability. But here too an instrument based solely on the naming of symptoms may be in danger of becoming too rigidly inflexible, a self-defining construction which cannot explore what it has been unable to name.

We feel that what we sometimes call proper scientific standards are defences we use to avoid getting involved with our patients in a dialogue bound to be coloured by our (and their) emotions and world-views. In this respect, Rowe (1980) writes:

> The psychiatrist too has his beliefs which affect how he structures his communication to the patient...Psychology and psychiatry have been very slow to learn what the physicists have known for many years—that the observer is always part of the experiment. Psychology and psychiatry have also been slow to realise that, while the nuclear particle may not be assessing the observer's inner effort to make sense of its environment, the human subject, the patient, is always engaged in trying to make sense of his individual world. Everything that comes into this world carries some communication.

It is true that papers discussing precipitant factors of schizophrenic behaviour refer to the social context of schizophrenia (Wing 1978b), to social environment and relapse in schizophrenia (Editorial *B.M.J.* 1980), or to crises and life changes preceding the onset or relapse of acute schizophrenia—clinical aspects (Birley and Brown 1970). Nevertheless, although acknowledging the influence of environmental factors on behaviour and emotional balance, this kind of research seems to take for granted that these factors have only an accessory role to play in the overall context of the officially accepted aetiopathogenic theory of schizophrenia. In fact, if we take into account the way these authors choose to present their facts and conclusions, we get the impression they continue to back (in line with traditional Jasperian viewpoints) a disease-process model of schizophrenia. In this model there is a place for the intervention of social and family factors but, as far as the true causes of schizophrenia are concerned, the role of these factors is very clearly limited (as Birley and Brown 1970 put it) to the mere precipitation of the acute onset, relapse or exacerbation of schizophrenic states.

Nevertheless, if we study these patients' biographies (and also our own lives and experiences) with the eyes of a novelist or historian, do we really have to postulate the existence of hypothetical disease processes in order to account for the mental state and behaviour of the disturbed people we call schizophrenic? Is not their situation much more akin to real life itself than we are usually inclined to admit? Perhaps the problems could be more meaningfully approached (and explained) as the ultimate result of the interaction between each patient's personality and his social environment. An interaction we could understand better if we were prepared to use our imagination and human concern. With its implicit acceptance of accessory social factors acting mechanically, as it were on the top of really important somatic causes (which nobody has so far managed to pinpoint), social psychiatry's conceptual model of schizophrenia has led both research workers and clinicians to ignore and/or dismiss the validity of alternative reticular and hierarchically fluctuating causality systems, to use again Joseph Needham's terminology.[1]

The empirical data provided by the recently organised International Pilot Study of Schizophrenia (World Health Organisation 1973) also call our attention to the pervasive influence exerted by psychosocial variables on the natural history of schizophrenia (that is on the biography of the disturbed and unhappy people we call schizophrenics). In fact, this research, although

1. See, for example, Day (1981) for a paradigmatic presentation of what we call here the mechanistic approach to socio-cultural factors in schizophrenia.

only possible after an agreement among researchers with regard to the basic requirements for the correct diagnosis of schizophrenia, has shown that the course and prognosis of the clinical cases thus selected varied largely from country to country, being more favourable in Third World nations than in European and particularly the Scandinavian countries.

Here we have a carefully designed study, aimed at demonstrating the existence of homogeneous disease entity (thought to have a probable organic origin), that ends up by showing the role played by socio-cultural factors with relation to the outcome of each patients' clinical history, or that the condition is not homogenous, in fact *reductio ad absurdum.*

The conclusions of the WHO study (1973) confirm the findings of research work done to compare the prognosis of cases of schizophrenia diagnosed, respectively, in countries of the Western world (Europe and North America) and in less industrialised and urbanised communities. Murphy and Raman (1971), for instance, wrote:

> One must apparently admit that the disorder [schizophrenia, that is] carries a much better prognosis in some indigenous tropical peoples than it does among Europeans, despite the better treatment available to the latter; and that our ideas regarding the chronicity of the disease may be wrong...Old ideas about schizophrenia being a 'disease of civilisation' then invite reassessment after they had apparently been laid to rest long ago.

After having found that the proportion of schizophrenic patients functioning normally and symptom-free on follow-up was higher in Mauritius than in British samples (and that the patients living in Mauritius had fewer relapses between discharge and follow-up than those in Britain), the authors explain their results in the following way:

> Our data suggest that if the disease is relatively mild, Mauritian conditions encourage the disappearance of symptoms whereas European conditions—or some of them at least—encourage their persistence. Where the disease is severe, on the other hand, neither set of conditions appears to make much difference... One possibility worth exploring is that the less affected European patient may be 'trapped' within an established sick role by the superficial rationality of his society's view of this sickness, whereas the Mauritian patient, with a range of what one could call superstitious explanations for his initial disorder, may more easily find a way of escape.

Obviously, we are far from agreeing with some of the concepts expressed in this paper or with the language these authors have used to characterise the clinical cases studied. Nevertheless, the basic facts concerning the course, prognosis and relapse rate of schizophrenia diagnosed in Britain and Mauritius, respectively, retain their significance and deserve attention. These facts show the complexity of the issues at stake in any meaningful discussion of schizophrenic behaviour.

In a more recent paper, Murphy and Taumorpean (1980) arrived at similar conclusions (see also Dale 1981). In an attempt to explain the better prognosis of schizophrenia in Tonga Islands (by comparison to Australia) these authors write:

> Turning now to the key differences between Tonga, as an example of a 'traditional society' and a 'modern' one, such as Australia, there are two differences which relate to what has just been said. In Tonga in the 1970s the average individual was provided with clear models for action insofar as he was expected to do mainly what his parents did before him, and insofar as the socio-economic situation enabled him to satisfy his own needs in this way. In Australia the average individual must cope with a host of procedures which his parents did not know and social pressures are less in favour of clinging to tradition than in favour of creating things new and original. Secondly, in Australia each individual is expected to compete with other individuals and take his own decisions; while in Tonga, although competitiveness in sport and sea-faring is encouraged, most decisions are taken communally (family, village, church, etc.) and the person who finds initiative difficult is not just permitted but encouraged to leave that to others. Accordingly, one might hypothesise that these features of Tonga life, ones which are found in some but by no means all other societies which we might call pre-industrial, protect the schizophrenia-prone individual from stresses which a more individualistic life-style would impose upon him.

Of course, the few papers we have quoted do not exemplify adequately the variety of issues that have been studied by social and transcultural psychiatry. Nevertheless, they offer an opportunity to reflect upon ways of conceptualising the reality of being mentally ill. What is in question, moreover, is not how shall we interpret the findings brought about by more or less exotic pieces of research but the more fundamental problem of the relations between psychiatry (defined as an area of specific professional expertise) and, on the other hand, the so-called human sciences (Davies 1981).

Perhaps as a result of the way the foundations of scientific psychiatry were laid down at the turn of the century (Scull 1981), the interchange of ideas and insights between psychiatrists and social scientists has been too scanty for a more imaginative conceptualisation of mental illness to be possible. We must not forget, however, that to practise social, transcultural, or anthropological psychiatry is not a matter of simply studying the precipitant factors of mental illness or travelling to distant and primitive places, but, as we see it, to fulfil our clinical duties having always in mind the wide range of social and cultural variables involved in any attempt to understand (and, if possible, modify) our patients' undesirable behaviour.

If we view schizophrenia as an undesirable variety of life process, social and cultural variables must certainly play an important role in the course and outcome of our patients' illnesses (or, to put it in other words, of their unique biographies).

Chapter 6

Neurobiological Research and the Question of the Cause of Schizophrenia

By the nature of the research we can guess what kind
of discovery the researcher can make.
Knowing this we can suspect that this discovery is what
the researcher secretly and unconsciously wants.

Gregory Bateson

Introduction

THE LATEST discoveries regarding brain biochemical processes and also the obvious (and often useful) clinical effects of psychopharmacological agents (such as the neuroleptic drugs) have been used by researchers and clinicians as strong arguments in favour of the neurobiochemical origin of schizophrenia. In this chapter we would like to try to demonstrate that this issue is much more complex than it seems and that the results of basic research methods cannot be used as overwhelmingly convincing evidence of the true nature and causes of schizophrenia.

Given the complexity of the human brain, in terms of functional circuits and chemical pathways (Brazier and Petsche 1978), we must exercise care if we want to avoid hasty interpretations of the hard facts that have been brought to light by basic brain research.

Trying to establish one analogy which we think could be paradigmatic we might recall that Einstein's Theory of Relativity implied the existence, until then unsuspected, of a correcting factor for the length, breadth and mass of an object which moves at a velocity (V) compared to the observer. As in physics, so in neurobiology we might need to reconsider our fundamental concepts when we analyse very complex phenomena which bring into play a great number of variables.

We suggest in this connection the following equation:

$$Q = n/N$$

n = number of factors in a conceptual model
N = number of cerebral neurones

where Q is *quotient of validity* of extrapolations from models to integrated cerebral action. This, of course, comes from the equations of relativity in which the length and other dimensions of objects depend on their velocity relative to the observer in relation to the velocity of light. For most relatively 'slow-moving' objects of our everyday world, Newtonian common sense is for all intents and purposes correct. Extrapolating, however, to different problems, that common sense is inadequate.

Newtonian physics is neither true nor false but only relevant to finite numbers of questions and purposes (Hesse 1974). We would choose to see psychiatric knowledge similarly, the questions are not matters of the excluded middle of Aristotle and they cannot be translated accurately from one to another paradigm; it remains up to us at what level we shall operate with reality which remains infinitely more subtle than our languages.

In biology the complexity of the interactions between phenomena and between the forms of auto-regulation and replication makes us question the concepts of natural laws and causality. They are in fact being progressively replaced by notions of systems, structures, models and processes. In line with this, aetiologies are not being sought in linear causal functions but in circular (even spiral) causal functions. There is an accepted inseparable dialectical relation between cause and consequence. This is the reason why in this field the search for cause is being replaced by looking for aims. So, in general in neurobiology and biology, deterministic linear causality is less acceptable. Its relevance is limited, even if it may be valid or at least useful in specific areas of scientific work (Bunge 1979), and other areas depend on complex probabilities. This is approximately and provisionally well portrayed in the concept of truth in science of Popper (1963), that it is in principle refutable conjecture so far resisting experimental refutation.

Obviously we would not like to delve into the interminable debate concerning the so-called mind-body relationships, although we think that on the whole psychiatrists have shown a considerable lack of philosophical sophistication whenever they have addressed themselves to the discussion of this matter (Hill 1981). Our aim is merely to enquire whether the facts we know in this field with a reasonable amount of confidence are (or are not) compatible with an interpretation of schizophrenia that chooses to emphasise its understandability and meaningfulness (that is, the basic intelligibility of what schizophrenic patients say or do).

Referring to schizophrenics' habitual perplexity and sense of social isolation, Jenner (1980) writes:

> If we play along with the games of the period we are classed as normal, but burning witches was once accepted by most. If we prefer to live in our own fantasy world we may not be accepted if we are also nuisances. We are then at war with others whose world we reject. We cannot fit into it. We have decided against conforming, we do not see it as in our interests. In such conflicts, and partly because of fear of submergence of our own independent selves, our ideas may run riot. But the patient, like all of us, needs to be a member of society. His problem is like the confusion of adolescence. Give in and be submerged, fight against and be stupidly alone. *Thinking about non-sensitized topics though, both the adolescent and the patient may show no confusion, which suggests that the brain is in working order.*

Critical Analysis of the Neurobiological Foundations of the Aetiology of 'Schizophrenia'

If we regard schizophrenics' behaviour and speech as self-defeating and undesirable kinds of lifestyle and interpersonal (mis)communication (Haley 1963), in a context of marked emotional distress and heightened concern with the 'self', we think it is by no means surprising to find in these deeply disturbed individuals: (a) neurobiochemical anomalies, probably qualitatively similar to those presented by normal people undergoing painful emotional experiences; (b) a positive therapeutic response to drugs whose main action consists in a chemical damping down of patients' highly increased state of arousal; (c) a pattern of psychophysiological reactions also suggesting a high level of central nervous system activation (or arousal).

Biochemical Aspects.

Concerning the neurobiochemical anomalies in schizophrenia, it is interesting to point out a commentary of Smythies (1963):

> Then, again, a possibility arises from this discussion that the metabolic disorders associated with schizophrenia, or at any rate some of them, may not be uniquely associated with clinical schizophrenia in any qualitative sense. They may occur in a lesser form in the metabolism of schizoid people, or in the metabolism of normal people undergoing complex and painful ego-damaging emotions, or even in the symptom-free relatives of schizophrenics. The chemical distinction between these groups may only be quantitative or regional. In the non-schizophrenics, the aberrant metabolic processes may never reach the pitch required to 'break bounds' and invade the whole cerebral mechanism of perception, thinking, emotional and motor control as they seem to do in schizophrenia.

Obviously, Smythies conceptualises schizophrenia in a way very different from our own. Nevertheless, he recognises that metabolic disorders similar to those possibly appearing in schizophrenia may also occur in normal people undergoing ego-damaging emotions.

The same can be said regarding the results obtained by means of recent 'neurobiological research' involving other kinds of strategy. For instance, the alterations in platelet monoamine-oxidase activity found in 'schizophrenic' patients (and previously thought to be related to possible 'basic aetiopathogenic mechanisms') are now known to be dependent on many types of variables having very little to do with the so-called 'schizophrenic disease process', such as drugs received by the patient, nutritional state, phase of the menstrual cycle, sex, and personality of the patient (Gattaz and Beckman 1981; Gattaz *et al.* 1981a), and, very curiously, levels of anxiety and arousal displayed by the patient (Mathew *et al.* 1981a). Mathew *et al.* (1981b: 372), for instance, wrote in this connection:

> The most important finding of this study is the significant decrease in platelet MAO activity after relaxation therapy... Evidence from other sources also supports an association between anxiety and MAO activity. It has been demonstrated that stress increases MAO activity in animals. Similarly, an association has been demonstrated between stress-related hormones such as ACTH and adrenaline and enzyme activity.
>
> Gentil and associates, and Owen and associates, demonstrated that injections of adrenaline increase platelet MAO activity in humans (cf. Bujatti and Riederer 1976).

In connection again with this kind of investigation, we think it is worthwhile to quote the following comments of Weiner (1983: 1129):

> At present it is generally conceded that low platelet levels of MAO occur only in some, not all, chronic schizophrenic patients. The various levels do not correspond with any particular type of schizophrenia... Some normal persons have levels that are even lower than those found in chronically schizophrenic patients...This conclusion—that the depressed levels are genetic markers—has been questioned (Dominic and Gahagan 1977). If this conclusion is correct, why should acutely schizophrenic patients have normal levels? And why do bipolar depressed patients also have low platelet levels? (cf. Bourdillon and Ridges 1971; Carlsson 1978; Heller *et al.* 1970; Hoffer 1967; Horrobin 1977; Horrobin 1980).

Very interesting findings have also come out in other fields of research. In the case of psychoendocrinology, for instance, Sachar (1970: 319-20) has elegantly demonstrated the existence of relationships between psychotic (and schizophrenic) intense emotional crises and adrenocortical responses of a massive and dramatic type. In a paper dealing with this type of research, this author writes:

> In this respect, the fixed delusion of the schizophrenic might be seen as a pathological psychological coping mechanism or defence, helping him to minimise anxiety in the same way that the profound religious faith of some of our women awaiting breast surgery helped them to maintain tranquillity. Indeed, as the schizophrenic patient in therapy gives up his delusions and faces painful reality again, he often re-experiences emotional distress and adrenal activation before he makes a full recovery... Certainly the diagnosis of schizophrenia alone will not tell us whether the adrenal cortex is activated or not. In these patients, it is necessary to isolate specifically the clinical dimensions of emotional arousal and disorganization of the ego's buffering mechanism.

As Rose, Kamin and Lewontin (1984) wrote:

> Most research is directed to a study of the biochemistry of the schizophrenic subjects themselves. Brain samples are rarely obtainable except post mortem, and so more readily accessible body materials—urine, blood or cerebrospinal fluid—from certified schizophrenics are compared with those from control normal people...
>
> When such approaches were first adopted several decades ago, they soon began to show up large differences in the biochemistry of hospitalised schizophrenic patients from those of normals matched for sex, age, and so forth. But these differences turned out to be artefactual; non-schizophrenic hospitalised patients showed similar differences from the normal. The differences were eventually traced to the effects of long periods of eating poor hospital diets, or to the chemical breakdown products of drugs that had been administered to the patients, or even to excessive coffee-drinking by hospitalised patients...
>
> It would be wearisome and unnecessary to recount in detail the history of research into the biochemistry of schizophrenia over the past thirty years. Almost every biochemical substance known to be present in the brain has, within two or three years of its introduction into the biochemical dictionary, been studied for possible involvement in schizophrenia by clinical scientists with the hope of a breakthrough in their hearts and with grant money (often from drug companies) burning holes in their pockets...
>
> Rarely have results obtained by one group of researchers been confirmed by another group of researchers in a different group of patients. Rarely has any resolution of conflicting claims been attempted. Rarely has any concern been expressed by the enthusiastic clinical researchers that schizophrenia might be associated with many different biochemical effects, or indeed that many different types of biochemical change might lead to or be generated by the same behavioural outcomes.

In addition to the above it seems worthwhile to consider other data presented in biochemical research reports on schizophrenia. The attempts to discover a biochemical basis for schizophrenia have not always been well executed. For example we can start from research which has seemed to reveal that patients have high serum copper levels. These were almost exclusively found in metal protein complexes. This is so as using the Akerfeld test confirmed that ceruloplasmin levels are also augmented in these patients. In these investigations several methodological mistakes were made (for example, the necessity to exclude situations in which high levels of ceruloplasmin occur, such as pregnancy and several diseases), and also obvious sources of technical errors since the test utilised is affected by serum levels of ascorbic acid (Weiner 1983). Hence the findings are related to other factors like the diet of patients. Further, the investigations of Bogoch (1960), which assert a low level of neuraminic acid in the C.S.F. of schizophrenics, may have suffered from influences hidden to the author, as they have not proved possible to repeat (see Jenner *et al.* 1962).

A line of research on abnormal levels of serum constituents was directed at proteins, especially some of them which are enzymes. Heath and Krupp (1968), for example, at Tulane University, carried out work on a protein fraction of the serum taraxein. This was identified as a circulating immunoglobulin, that is, an antibody with the capacity to interact by ligation to the nucleus of oligodendrocite of the septal area of the cerebrum. It is said to be produced by an inborn error of metabolism. These findings have, however, not so far been confirmed (Boehme *et al.* 1973; Logan and Deodhar 1970; Whittingham *et al.* 1968).

Recently works have appeared on the levels of immunoglobulins of schizophrenics. Solomon *et al.* (1969) reported elevations of IgG in one of several studies of various subgroups of immunoglobulins (A-D-G-M). Yet this has not been confirmed by other workers. The elevated levels of serum IgM, reported in other works, now seem to be related to administration of psychotropic drugs.

Haddon and Rabe found in 1963 an abnormal antigen in the serum of schizophrenic patients. Subsequent work (Rosenblatt *et al.* 1968; Solomon *et al.* 1969) identified a rheumatoid factor in the serum of these patients. They did not, however, correlate with a diagnosis of schizophrenia but with depressed mood. None of this has been confirmed by Mellsop *et al.* (1973).

In 1968 Burch *et al.* proposed a conceptualisation of the pathogenesis of schizophrenia as an autoimmune disease. Even if it is definite that the existence of a rheumatoid factor is an autoimmune phenomenon in which IgG acquires antigenic properties,[1] which by themselves develop antibodies, it is also true that the presence of these antibodies does not necessarily give them a pathogenic role in any disease. They can occur in normal individuals. Some works of less impact (Pulkinnen 1977; Stabenau *et al.* 1968; Turner and Chipps 1966) reported other immunological reactions but all are without any conclusive findings.

Research on altered levels of enzymes in the blood of acute psychotic patients has been directed at several categories of substances, although we can only emphasise the most widely studied, for example creatinine-phosphokinase (CPK), aldolase and the monoaminoxidases (MAOS). The elevation of the serum transaminase glutamine oxaloacetic acid oxidase (TGO)

1. This antigenic property possibly results from a genetic mutation in immunocompetent cells.

encountered by Schweid *et al.* (1972) has not been confirmed by other investigations.

Elevated levels of CPK in a certain percentage (c. 40%) of patients with a wide spectrum of acute psychoses (Coffey *et al.* 1970; Meltzer 1976) has also been confirmed. However, in most of the cases levels returned to normal some days or weeks following the onset of the episode. Further, it has been found that enzyme alterations depend on a number of factors, such as race, sex (Meltzer *et al.* 1973) and the intramuscular injections (Meltzer 1969; Meltzer and Moline 1970a). Significantly the iso-enzyme of CPK which is elevated in acute psychoses is of muscle origin and not cerebral (Meltzer 1969; Meltzer and Moline 1970b) and the same is so for aldolase. In this way the elevated serum levels of CPK and aldolase found mainly in the initial phase of the 'diseases' are not specific for schizophrenia and we cannot discern what, if anything, that can mean for an aetiological theory of schizophrenia. Harding (1974) says, when other variables are controlled, the serum enzyme levels reflect an increase in motor activity and not the psychotic disease itself. This seriously puts in doubt the diagnostic validity and predictive value of CPK and aldolase levels in schizophrenia.

Another line of research is based on a view that the pathogenesis of schizophrenia is provoked by abnormal metabolites with psychotomimetic properties but resulting from normal body constituents. In this context it has been suggested that 3,4-dimethoxyphenylethylamine (Friedhoff and Van Winkle 1962a) originates from endogenous dopamine, or exogenous diet, but a correlation between its levels and the diagnosis of schizophrenia (Mendolson 1964) has not been clearly shown. For a long time the correct gas chromatographic mass spectrographic identification in urine was also in question. Dimethyltryptamine originating via a hypothetic abnormal metabolic pathway has also been investigated, but it has not been shown to be specific for schizophrenia.

It was the work of Osmond *et al.* (1952) on transmethylation disorders producing psychotomimetic substances which became entangled with the pink spot story. Friedhoff and Van Winkle (1962) reported a pink spot on paper chromatograms treated with specific reagents (ninhydrin followed by Ehrlich's reagent) which seemed to be specific for schizophrenia. Bourdillon *et al.* (1965) took this very seriously indeed and seemed unaware of the tendentious nature of schizophrenia and the problems of chemical studies in this field. They intended, taking genetic theories as facts, to use the spot as a marker. They reported 46 positive findings from 73 schizophrenics and none from 16 non-schizophrenics. This apparent confirmation of the more limited report of Friedhoff and Van Winkle (1962), the theorising of Osmond *et al.* (1952), and the fact that a similarly reacting spot is produced by 3,4, dimethoxyphenylethylamine, a methylated product of dopamine, made a great story, all fitting together. Similar spots can, however, be produced by many substances. Yet again, the so-convincing turns out to be the artefacts produced by enthusiasm rather than careful and accurate science. This story teaches many lessons about the traps for the unwary and enthusiastic scientist. The history of research into schizophrenia is full of such stories.

However, an English referee of this book pointed out:

> The main difficulty [of publishing this book] is that the people to whom it is addressed will not read it precisely because it challenges their training and practice. A Catch-22. You will no doubt be familiar with the cries of the majority of biologically-orientated psychiatrists that with so many patients to see every day *how can they find the time to understand them*?—they are *forced* to *palliate symptoms* only.

It might be added that if we knew the genetic problems it would anyway be better to manipulate the genes.

It is difficult not to report a work in which samples from sweat coming from schizophrenic and control persons interned in the same hospital were studied. Smith and Sines (1960) 'demonstrated' the existence of the peculiar smell of the sweat from a great number of schizophrenic patients. They maintained further that laboratory mice could be conditioned to discriminate in a significant way the smell from the sweat extracted from each one of the groups of studied patients. Using the results of this study, in which the basic material conditions of the institutional life and nourishment were not taken into account, lots of psychiatrists allowed themselves to be seduced by the usefulness of that peculiar smell as a diagnostic criterion for schizophrenia.

It is interesting to recall the famous *faetor judaicus*, a particular kind of fetidness that, from classical antiquity up to the seventeenth century, some educated people and inquisitors noticed in Jews. For Father Cristovaeo de Santo Tirso, the generation of Jews was as fetid as were their errors. The case becomes more complicated when Vincente da Costa in 1668 in Lisbon assured that the baptised Jews lost the fetidness of their bodies but that they regained their particular smell as soon as they apostatised the Christian religion. He explained: 'some serious doctors say that this fetidness was natural in all those who participated in Our Lord's death' (cf. Sampeio Bruno 1983). Therefore there is reason to remark that at the time genetical theories about such a smell already prevailed, even though the genetic imperfections could be manipulated by religious means.

At present no confirmation of theories depending on tryptamine (Domino and Gahagan 1977), methionine (Pollin *et al.* 1961), and tryptophan has been produced, nor of the alterations of nitrogen metabolism which have received the attention of some authors (Gjessing 1947).

Whether the published biochemical anomalies described are the cause of schizophrenia, or are co-variants of the psychological or behavioural state of schizophrenic patients, is the question that Weiner (1983: 1147-49) discusses when he writes:

> One cannot help wondering how the finding of a specific biochemical substance, for instance, would enhance the understanding of the cause of schizophrenia. Presumably, such a substance could be important as a validating criterion of diagnosis, in the manner that changed levels of the thyroid hormones serve as a validating diagnostic criterion of thyroid diseases. But such a finding would have little aetiological significance in itself, because the causes of the diseases of the thyroid gland are largely unknown and go far beyond changes in the levels of the thyroid hormones. Furthermore, changes in a substance or substances may be co-variants of some behavioural manifestation...
>
> Logic dictates that a pathophysiological finding is not necessarily pathogenic, despite the traditional attempts in medicine to attempt to infer causes and pathogenesis from pathophysiology and pathological anatomy after the start of an illness. Knowledge of the causes and pathogenesis of all illness is limited and will be advanced only by predictive and longitudinal studies of persons at risk for a particular illness and its subforms.

Psychopharmacology and Psychosurgery.

The advances in psychopharmacological research cannot be denied. They attest to the success of a specific type of approach to the problems of mental ill-health. It is also true that the method of looking at disturbed peolple implied by this kind of research strategy is taken for granted as the only correct one. Yet one can forget the intrinsic drawbacks (secondary effects, naive and too confident use of psychopharmacotherapy, etc.) and the fact that the reality of mental disorder is in itself problematic, requiring an open mind ready to envisage several ways of world-making. The apparent successes of a certain clinical approach (in this case the well-known pharmacological effects of neuroleptic drugs in schizophrenia) can lock the doctor in a rigid stance, closely linked with his theories of causality. This short-sighted attitude lessens the creative powers of the psychiatrist, blocking his therapeutic potential.

Baldessarini (1985: 387-88) makes some comments which in our opinion all psychiatrists should read:

> Antipsychotic drugs exert beneficial effects in virtually all classes of psychotic illness and, contrary to a common misconception, are not selective for schizophrenia...Thus the hopes of the 1950s and 1960s for the discovery of clearly defined, genetically determined inborn errors of the metabolism to explain psychiatric disease have not been realised.
>
> Moreover, there is a growing realisation that there may be an over-

> simplification in the attempt to formulate hypotheses about the causes of mental illness from the tenets of psychopharmacology. Thus it was commonly hoped that knowledge of the mechanisms of action of antipsychotic or anti-depressant drugs would point the way to the discovery of underlying patho-physiological changes in schizophrenia or manic-depressive illness that are functionally opposite to the effects of the drugs. This has not proved to be the case.
>
> The antipsychotic, antimanic and anti-depressant drugs have effects on cortical, limbic, hypothalamic and brain stem mechanisms that are of fundamental importance for the regulation of arousal, consciousness, affect and autonomic functions. It is entirely possible that physiological and pharmacological modification of these brain regions might have important behavioural consequences and useful clinical effects regardless of the fundamental nature or cause of the mental disorder in question. Moreover, the relatively poor temporal correlations between the known effects of most psychotropic drugs, which for the most part occur rapidly, and their clinical effects suggest that secondary or even more indirect changes brought about by the drugs may mediate their clinical actions.

In the case of schizophrenia, there is an average latency interval of about three weeks between the beginning of treatment and the appearance of the therapeutic results, as far as schizophrenia's typical psychopathology is concerned—as delusions, hallucinations and formal thought disorders are probably a result of a state of increased arousal (and emotional turmoil) they will only begin to fade out after patients' anxiety has been damped down by these drugs to a reasonably low level (Klein 1981; May 1971; May 1973).

The dopaminergic theory of the aetiology of schizophrenia proposes an abnormally high level of dopamine or an increased post-synaptic sensitivity to dopamine. The hypothesis arose in part from an extrapolation of the mode of action of the neuroleptic drugs proposed by Carlsson and Lindquist in 1962. They showed that in mice brains neuroleptics increased the levels of the metabolites of dopamine, suggesting therefore that they had blocked the dopaminergic receptors. These suggestions have been impressively confirmed by subsequent and more sophisticated techniques.

In this connection, Weiner (1983: 1147) writes:

> From the known actions of the drugs, a hypothesis is constructed about the case and the pathogenesis of schizophrenia. But is this a logical approach to its cause and pathogenesis? The pharmacological action of a drug like digitalis in congestive heart failure does not tell us about the multivarious reasons why the heart failed. Many drugs with a variety of pharmacological actions on different systems are used for the treatment of essential hypertension, whose cause and pathogenesis are quite unknown. At best the action of a drug may indicate

> something about the pathophysiology of a disease but not about its predisposition or inception. In fact it may even be dangerous to extrapolate from the action of a drug to the pathophysiology of a disease.

Illustrating this same point, Rose, Kamin and Lewontin (1984: 218) wrote:

> Drugs that alleviate symptoms, like the use of aspirin for toothache, may be worth developing even if they tell nothing about the causes of the disorder. The multiplicity of drugs (and formulations of drugs) is an aspect of the way the pharmaceutical companies work in a field where knowledge of patent law is as important as clinical skills. The problem is that of confounding the effect of a drug with the offer of an explanation, the alleviation of suffering with a cure for the disease.

Accepting this view the therapeutic efficacy of a drug does not allow us to draw clear conclusions about the aetiopathogenesis of a disease. It is not in itself an adequate basis for such a conclusion. In this respect there is a difficulty in determining what is so before or only after the onset of a pathological state, and that limits the power to produce a conclusive aetiopathology.

These obstacles to causal investigations of schizophrenia led to utilising research strategies based on experimental induction of model psychoses, by the so-called psychotomimetic drugs like amphetamine, mescaline and LSD 25. Rose, Kamin and Lewontin (1984: 217) comment on this strategy:

> Such problems have made yet another approach more attractive to reductionist thinking; to observe the effects of pharmacological agents—drugs—on human behavior. If a drug induces schizophrenia-like behavior—for example, auditory hallucinations—then attempts will be made to conclude that the drug interferes with a biochemical process in the normal person which is damaged in the schizophrenic. Hence, for example, there was a period in the 1960s in which attempts were made to find links between LSD and schizophrenia on the grounds that users of LSD experienced hallucinations that might be seen as analogous to those of the schizophrenic. This logic, which argues backwards from the effect of a drug to the cause of a disease (*ex juvantibus* logic) (Bogoch 1960) is plainly risky, both for the logician and the patient. As we have emphasised in the case of L-dopa, no drug has a single site of action. Foreign chemicals introduced into the body are not magic bullets. Yet such thinking has dominated more than thirty years of research on the biochemistry of schizophrenia, generated endless research papers, made scientific and medical reputations, and brought substantial profit to the big drug firms. The history of thinking among biochemists about schizophrenia over the period is inextricably intertwined with that of the pharmaceutical industry, for which psychotropic drugs have been one of the biggest money spinners.

Iversen (1981), for instance, summarising the results of his painstaking research of the biochemical mechanisms of schizophrenia, has recently proclaimed the 'death of the dopamine-hypothesis'. He implied with this statement that we should begin to search elsewhere for the causes of schizophrenia since his findings (as far as dopamine was concerned) did not confirm the role of this amine as an aetiological factor in schizophrenia. As a biochemist he might, of course, continue his search for other possible neuro-biochemical explanations, although we think we are also entitled to approach this problem from a different perspective.

Even before the appearance of neuroleptics, writers, including the eminent Portuguese neurologist, Egas Moniz (1874–1955) in 1935, identified the organic basis of thought in the synapses. He tried to deduce from the therapeutic effects of pre-frontal lobotomy, for which discovery he won the Nobel Prize in 1949, that certain psychoses, including schizophrenia, were caused by abnormal brain function. Szasz (1977) commented on this inference that Moniz recognised that his objective in applying lobotomy to human beings was less to find a cure for psychoses than it was to lay the corner stone for the edifice of organic psychiatry. That was to establish a firm basis for an organic theory of the functional psychoses. Citing the work of Egas Moniz is not to condemn him but to illustrate why this type of investigation is unlike traditional medical research. In order to establish the organic nature of dementia paralytica, the medical research workers studied post mortem brains. Hence they established the histopathological nature of the condition. They had not tried to prove that G.P.I. was an organic disease mutilating the body, nor draw conclusions from the therapeutic intervention about the nature of the disease. The reasoning behind the method of Egas Moniz is widely accepted today. For instance it is generally believed that because the major tranquillisers affect behaviour in ways many feel is desirable, this proves that the patients have a disease with an organic base. These ideas of Szasz do more than reinforce the thoughts of Baldessarini which were presented at the beginning of this chapter.

Psychophysiology and Neurophysiology.

Apropos of psychophysiological studies applied to schizophrenia, it is interesting to note that much which is portrayed as new is misleading because suitable control groups have not been studied.

Lader (1975) writes in this respect:

> Practically all the positive findings in schizophrenics have also been described in anxiety states whenever direct comparisons have been made. It is not defeatism but realism to suggest that no psychophysiological property of schizophrenics has been unequivocally demonstrated. Until patients with

> anxiety states are routinely included as an additional control in studies of schizophrenic patients no real scientifically sound conclusions can be drawn. Thus, the raised autonomic and endocrine variables, the lack of reactivity, the slowness to adapt and habituate, the poor stimulus discrimination and the generally impaired performance of the schizophrenic are found to a greater or lesser extent in the morbidly anxious patient and can often be induced by stressful procedures in the calm normal (cf. Toone *et al.* 1981).

In the field of neurophysiological research, the findings obtained by workers who have studied neurotic (and, therefore supposedly understandable) patients are reported. Ciesielski *et al.* (1981), for instance, were able to find significant differences (as regards certain kinds of evoked potentials) between obsessional patients and matched normal controls. Hoffmann and Goldstein (1981: 159) also managed to prove the existence of what they called hemispheric quantitative E.E.G. changes in neurotic patients showing symptoms of tension, anxiety and/or depression. These same quantitative E.E.G. changes seemed to be responsive to certain kinds of psychotherapeutic intervention, mainly in the case of patients who had been rated as very anxious during the psychotherapy sessions (high intensity group). These authors suggest that the E.E.G. changes found in the high intensity group, following a therapy session, reflect a general deactivation of the brain and a functional improvement of the right hemisphere. In another passage, they present the hypothesis that the release of blocked feelings in a primal therapy session is followed by an overall increase in both E.E.G. amplitude and amplitude variance in the temporal areas indicating a more relaxed (less activated) brain.

It has been suggested by Holzman *et al.* in 1973 that a risk factor is associated with abnormal occulomotor tracking. This was confirmed by others (Shagass *et al.* 1974; Shagass *et al.* 1976) and used as a genetic marker for schizophrenia (Holzman *et al.* 1977). However, it is subject to similar objections to those of other works we have cited.

Weiner (1983: 1130) writes:

> The abnormality is present in non-schizophrenic persons and in the relatives of schizophrenic patients...It may be premature to ask the meaning of such abnormalities... Does it reflect some central neural state that impairs attention or the sampling of the appearance of the external world? But why should an impairment lead to schizophrenia in some and not in others? And why does the disorder persist in remitted schizophrenic patients? Brain disease can produce the same dysfunction. It is seen in cerebral arteriosclerosis, Parkinson's disease, lesions of the brain stem and cerebral hemispheres, and psychotically depressed patients.

Conclusion

Just as Rose, Lewontin and Kamin (1984: 218) submit, we think that:

> Among the claims for causative factors in schizophrenia made since the 1950s we may point to: abnormal substances excreted in the sweat of schizophrenics; injection of the serum of schizophrenics into other normal subjects inducing abnormal behavior; and the presence of abnormal enzymes in red blood cells and blood proteins. Between 1955 and the present day, conflicting research reports have claimed that schizophrenia is caused by disorders in serotonin metabolism (1955); noradrenaline metabolism (1971); dopamine metabolism (1972); acetylcholine metabolism (1973); endorphin metabolism (1976); and prostaglandin metabolism (1977). Some molecules, such as the amino acids glutamate and gamma-amino-butyric acid, came into fashion in the late 1950s, but fell into neglect, and now, in the 1980s, have come back into fashion once more.

As well as the works described, many others have been devoted to schizophrenia. Without pretence of being exhaustive, we could include studies of histamine, reduced susceptibility to infections, the alterations of glucose metabolism and relations to other diseases (for example, tuberculosis, hereditary disorders and neurological diseases: porphyria, homocystinura, Huntington's Chorea, Wilsons's disease, etc.).

In our opinion, what all these studies appear to indicate is that the finding of (more or less conspicuous) neurobiochemical, psychophysiological, psychoendrocrinological, or neurophysiological anomalies (when we proceed to study the workings of the human brain) does not necessarily imply the existence of any sort of disease process (which could therefore be the only one capable of producing the anomalies).

So the eventual discovery even of an enzyme defect in schizophrenia does not necessarily imply that this is genetically determined, nor that it has a specific causal relation to schizophrenia. With this in mind it is interesting to quote further Rose, Kamin and Lewontin (1984: 212):

> At an earlier time psychiatrists and neurologists chose to distinguish between organic and functional nervous disorders...But such a distinction is unacceptable to the dominant, full-blooded materialism of contemporary psychiatry. If there is a disordered mind, there must be associated with it some type of disordered molecular or cellular event in the brain. Further, the reductionist argument insists that there must be a direct causal chain running from the molecular events in particular brain regions to the most full-blown manifestations of existential despair suffered by the individual
>
> Even when proper care is taken to circumvent this problem by ensuring that the subjects studied have been kept off drugs for a period, that they have the

> same diet as their matched controls, and so forth, there remains a general methodological problem that cannot be avoided. Even if an abnormal chemical is found in the body fluids of a diagnosed schizophrenic compared with the best-matched of controls, one cannot infer that the observed substance is the cause of schizophrenia; it might instead be a consequence. The causal argument assumes that the substance is present, and, as a result, the disorder begins. A consequential argument says that first the disorder occurs and then as a result the substance accumulates. If an individual suffers an infection from a flu virus there is a considerable increase in the antibodies present in the blood and mucus of the nose—they are the body's defence mechanisms against the virus. The antibodies and the mucus haven't caused the infection and one cannot readily deduce the actual causes simply by observing such consequences...
>
> The ideology of biological determinism is linked to an insistence that biological events are ontologically prior to and cause the behavioural or existential events, and hence to a claim that if brain biochemistry is altered in schizophrenia, then underlying this altered biochemistry must be some type of genetic predisposition to the disorder.

These same anomalies can also be found, as we have seen in the case of neurotic patients and (as far as psychotic patients are concerned) no data so far obtained go against them being explained within a psychodynamically understandable model, one that takes into account psychotic patients' motives and purposes and tries not to forget the meaning of their symptoms.

After decades of intensive investigations the following seems a valid comment of Szasz (1977): 'although we have mountains of facts about neurochemistry and psychopharmacology we have none about schizophrenia'.

It is perhaps worthwhile to conclude this chapter with the following comments of Weiner (1983: 1147) about the neurobiological investigation of schizophrenia:

> The information reviewed, however, points up another common fallacy in schizophrenia research—the role of fashion in dictating research and hypothesis construction. As Snyder *et al.* (1974) pointed out: 'Why should nature have chosen to inflict the "schizophrenic abnormality" upon whatever specific chemical the experimentalist happens to be best equipped to measure?'

Chapter 7

The Genetic Basis of Schizophrenia?

To attribute a part of our totality to heredity and the rest to the environment doesn't make sense. It is like asking how much of the affection of Romeo for Juliet has a genetic or cultural origin.

Francois Jaçob

Introduction

THE FINDINGS of psychiatric genetics have been frequently used by researchers and clinicians alike as a means of proving the hereditary basis of schizophrenia and the reasonableness of the theories that ascribe to this mental disorder the status of a specific and discrete nosological entity with a (most probable) organic basis.

However, the lack of reliable external criteria for the validation of the clinical diagnosis of schizophrenia has put research workers in the curious position of having to investigate the genetic basis of a disease without being certain about what they mean when they speak about that same disease. It is true that clinicians and researchers have been able to reach some agreement among themselves with regard to the conventional definition of schizophrenia. We must not forget, however, that these conventional entities (see, for example, WHO 1973) are often taken for granted as real or objective things. This is a misleading way of thinking and is bound to distort the interpretation and ultimate significance of research data.

A Critical Review of Research Work on the Genetic Basis of Schizophrenia

With the passage of time several strategies have been used to identify the role of the transmission of genetic factors in schizophrenia (Fonseca 1965). These have included family trees, consanguinity, twin studies, adoption studies and linkage studies.

In this connection, however, we cannot but recognise that much has changed since the heroic times of Rudin, Kallman and Luxenburger as far as research methodologies and theories conceptualising the role of genetic factors in schizophrenia are concerned. As Revely and Murray (1980) put it:

> Many of the methodological and environmentalist criticisms were assimilated by geneticists into important refinements of the twin and family studies, including the examination of reared-part twins. In addition, the adoptive strategy was introduced to tease apart genes and environment by studying individuals who received their genes from one set of parents but their upbringing from another.

Family studies only confirm that schizophrenia can be familial. Many things run in families, everything from eating habits to healthy behaviours, without being genetically determined since families share lifestyles as well as genes. Since the different aspects of the acquisition of behaviour imply either genetic or cultural transmission, the results of consanguinity studies are not conclusive proof of the inheritance of schizophrenia (Kinney 1983).

It is evident that the striking results obtained by 'pioneer' research workers in the field of psychiatric genetics (for instance, the family and twin studies produced by Kallmann 1938) were contaminated by methodological mistakes. They have been consistently contradicted by more recent (and sophisticated) research programmes and current ideas concerning the genetic transmission of schizophrenia are much less straightforward (and naive) than forty or fifty years ago.

On the history of psychiatric genetics, Gershon (1981: 274) wrote:

> His (Kallmann's) first major work, published after his arrival in the United States, was a family study of schizophrenia in 13,851 relatives of 1,087 patients admitted to a Berlin hospital in a ten-year period, in which he estimated the prevalences of the different forms of schizophrenia in relatives of patients compared with the general population. The population expectancy of 0.85% was much smaller than the expectancy in relatives of 16.4% (children) and 11.5% (siblings). This implied the hereditary nature of schizophrenia, although cultural transmission of schizophrenia was not ruled out until the Danish–American adoption studies a generation later.

Without denying the obvious methodological superiority of the Danish-American adoption studies (Kety *et al.* 1971; Rosenthal *et al.* 1971) over, for instance, the pioneer research work of Kallmann, these studies cannot, in our opinion, be accepted as providing conclusive evidence in favour of the role of clear-cut genetic factors in the aetiology of schizophrenia.

Considering the study of adopted-away offspring of schizophrenics, it becomes clear that the difference between index (offspring of schizophrenics) and control (offspring of normal biological parents) adoptees in regard to the incidence of schizophrenia, is statistically significant only if we include in the group of 76 index adoptees 24 people whose biological parents were diagnosed either as manic-depressive patients or as psychiatric patients suffering from a variety of disturbances but not from schizophrenia spectrum disorders.

Lidz *et al.* (1981: 1066) call our attention to this same point:

> If one excludes these 13 non-schizophrenic index parents (the parents who had been previously diagnosed as manic-depressive patients) and their 6 'spectrum' children from the data, the difference between the index and control group is no longer statistically significant (x^2 = 2.079, df = 1, one tailed p = .075, n.s.). The inclusion of the 11 index parents with very indefinite diagnoses (the judges could not agree which diagnosis applied) further obscures the findings.

> With the exclusion of the 13 index subjects with manic-depressive psychoses and the 11 index subjects with indefinite diagnoses, none of whom properly belongs in a study of the adopted-away offspring of schizophrenic parents, the difference between the index and control series does not even approach statistical significance ($x^2 = 0.92$, df = 1, one tailed p = .50, n.s.).

This study fails, therefore, to replicate Heston's findings (Heston 1966, 1970), which had been widely accepted as strong evidence in favour of the hypothesis that schizophrenia is essentially a genetic disorder and which suggested a so-called common-core diathesis for schizophrenia and sociopathy.

Heston studied 47 offspring who had been permanently separated from their hospitalised schizophrenic mothers in the first few months of life and compared them with the offspring of 50 non-schizophrenic mothers who were also separated at a very early age. He found that 5 children of the schizophrenic mothers had become schizophrenic, in contrast to none of the controls, and his index series also contained 9 sociopaths (control series–2), 13 neurotics (control series–7), and 4 mentally defective individuals (control series–0).

However, Heston's index subjects were offspring of hospitalised schizophrenic mothers, a fact which may have blocked favourable adoption conditions, and some of these subjects were actually raised in institutions. Being born in a psychiatric hospital from a schizophrenic mother is most probably prejudicial to the offspring's future adaptation to the social world and this for a variety of reasons (physical and psychosociological) that have very little to do with the hypothetical genes of schizophrenia.

It is interesting to notice that Heston's index group has also a significantly higher number of sociopaths and mentally defective individuals by comparison with the control group (9/2 and 4/0, respectively). In our opinion, instead of having to postulate a hypothetical common-core diathesis for schizophrenia and sociopathy (this says nothing about mental deficiency), it would have been more reasonable to ascribe these interesting differences to the fact that the index adoptees were brought up in less favourable conditions (including their intra-uterine period of development) which must have contributed to their greater proneness to a variety of psychiatric disorders (Wolkind 1979).

We must not forget that the child of a schizophrenic mother may well have to face its substitute parents (and the world at large) with an underweight and tiny body (Humphrey 1980: 297) as well as with a tainted pedigree. It is interesting that one of Heston's five schizophrenic index adoptees was also diagnosed as mentally defective a long time before the onset of his schizophrenic disease and was given an IQ of 62. Smith (1980: 352) drew our attention to this kind of problem when he wrote:

> I was recently involved in the adoption of the baby of a sixteen-year-old schizophrenic whose own mother had also suffered from schizophrenia. The social workers explained that the adopting parents were entitled to the background information about the baby's origins and I agreed to meet them. Questions were asked about the heritability of schizophrenia and even what signs to look out for in adolescence in the unfortunate event that the daughter should develop the illness. I realised that the child entered its family trailing a background of schizophrenia and would be watched closely all its life to see if the hereditary taint would show itself in abnormality. What is the bearing of this on the adoption research from Oregon and Denmark (see Gottesmar 1978), which I had thought represented cast iron evidence for schizophrenia being to a substantial extent truly inherited by genetic mechanisms? If there was some transmission of background information to the adopting parents, as can occur in this country, did it invalidate the aim of the research to separate genetic and environmental influences on the children studied?

The Scandinavian studies of Fischer (1973) show the incidence rate of schizophrenia, corrected for age, in the offsprings of each monozygotic (MZ) twin of a pair discordant for the disease is identical (10%). This leads us to conclude that genetic transmission alone is not adequate to explain the origin of the cases of schizophrenia in these offsprings.

The claims of the authors of the second Danish–American study (Kety *et al.* 1971) to have proved beyond reasonable doubt the genetic basis of schizophrenia have also been successfully challenged by a few research workers. Benjamin (1976: 1131), for instance, wrote in this connection:

> In this study there was a highly significant difference between 'index' and 'control' groups in the half-sibling category, and there were no clear differences in the full-sibling or parent categories. This finding is peculiar and contradictory. It shows, in effect, that the less the consanguinity, the greater the genetic effect. Differences should be weakest, not strongest, in the half-sibling category.

In the same paper, Benjamin (1976: 1132) pointed to another very interesting question which in our opinion has much to do with the methodological issues brought about by the comparative studies of index and control groups in the field of psychiatric genetics:

> Although the interpretative assumption of the authors was that differences are associated with poor (destructive, defective, illness-inducing) genes in the index group, it is equally possible that observed differences could also be associated with good (constructive, superior) genes in the control group. For example, those who think of schizophrenia as a maladaptive social solution to problems in living might argue that the control adoptees without any psychiatric history had more genetically determined social assets, such as better physical

> appearance, intelligence, athletic ability and/or other talents that can facilitate optimal social adjustment in Western culture...Since the study failed to match the biological families of index and control groups for genetically based social assets, it could be that control adoptees without psychiatric histories tended to come from middle and upper class persons with favourable genetic heritage who were giving up infants for adoption because of illegitimate teenage pregnancies, whereas index adoptees tended to have been put up for adoption because of more chaotic social situations characteristic of persons with less genetic (and environmental) advantage in social adaptation. However, this formulation, like the genetic interpretation, falters because of the failure to find differences between the index and control groups. Thus the argument remains at a stalemate.

The same situation of stalemate can be said to exist with regard to the findings so far brought about by twin studies. Both theoretical critiques and empirical research have clearly demonstrated that earlier twin studies produced results that greatly overestimated the role of genetic factors in schizophrenia. More recent investigations which have attempted to avoid the pitfalls of unrepresentative sampling and uncertain zygosity diagnosis have arrived at considerably lower concordance rates in MZ twins with respect to schizophrenia.

Although the higher concordance for schizophrenia of MZ twins is not an artefact, its significance is complex. The definitive conclusion from the fact that the concordance level is about 50% is that the environment must have a role (Kinney 1983). Jackson (1960) emphasised the particular environment of MZ twins. They are often dressed in the same way, mistaken in their identity, treated as 'the twins' and not individually, and they share common experiences (Koch 1966). Also pre- and perinatal environments were similar, and they can contribute to the high concordance levels between MZ twins. In MZ twins discordant for schizophrenia, obstetric difficulties are commoner in the psychotic twins (McNeil and Kaij 1978; Pollin and Stabenau 1968). Studies not involving twins have also shown higher level of obstetric complications in patients than in controls, which included normal brothers (McNeil and Kaij 1978) and adopted children (Jacobsen and Kinney 1980). The MZ twins, as compared to dizygotic (DZ) twins, show lower birth weight as well as other developmental differences, such as retarded intra-uterine development, elevated levels of early mortality and perinatal morbidity (Campion and Tucker 1973).

In twin studies there are several sources of error which makes comparisons between MZ and DZ twins problematical and which cannot be overcome. (For example, the genetic repertoire of each of the MZ pair differs in the way in which the environment induces the activation of the genes, and in the timing of the activation of these inductions during the critical periods of development). In other words, it is clear that MZ and DZ twins do not present to us perfect natural experiments.

The second Danish–American study (Kety *et al.* 1971) attempted to avoid the limitations already cited. In this second study the majority of the sons of schizophrenic parents had been adopted before the first psychotic episode of the parents. This eliminates the pre- and perinatal environmental factor following the parents' disease. It also overcomes the criticism in Heston's study about the influence of the knowledge of the mental disease of the biological mother on the disease of the adopted child. Nevertheless, this study also produced the contradictory results which we have indicated. These will be further analysed in the concluding part of this chapter.

The linkage between schizophrenia and a hypothetical genetic marker could be favourable to a genetic theory. The studies so far performed by several authors (Asarnow 1978; Demish *et al.* 1977; Holzman *et al.* 1980; Turner 1979; Wyatt *et al.* 1975) do not elucidate whether such markers are of discrete alleles predisposing to schizophrenia, or pleotropic effects (Kety and Kinney 1981; Kinney 1983). We must mention, among others, the following studies: linkage between schizophrenic spectrum disorders and the genes responsible for the HLA antigens for histocompatibility (Turner 1979).

In our opinion the investigations of linkage and biological indicators of schizophrenia lead to speculations about the precipitating role of the altered enzymatic levels. These thoughts are, however, undermined by the fact that the enzymes are not exclusively under the control of the genes. There are suggestions that enzymatic levels in the brain and the organism in general are influenced by earlier social experiences (Henry *et al.* 1971; Stone *et al.* 1976). A metabolic error, like that of phenylketonuria, is only clinically demonstrable if phenylalanine is present in the diet. In other words, the enzymatic defect in phenylketonuria predisposes to but is not sufficient for its occurrence. So the eventual discovery of an enzymatic defect in schizophrenia might not necessarily mean that such a defect or deviation is genetically determined or has a simple causal relation to schizophrenia. This suggests that the disease might not be genetically transmitted even if the predisposition is.

Despite the fact that most authors agree that there is no simple genetic transmission of schizophrenia (Stone *et al.* 1976; Kidd and Cavalli-Storza 1973; Matthyssi and Kidd 1976; Shields *et al.* 1975; Slater and Cowie 1971), there is not any agreement about the hypothetical mode of genetic transmission of the condition. Several models have been proposed:

a. A monogenetic or monofactorial theory. These theories respectively involve (i) a recessive gene modified or not in its action on other genes and with the heterozygotes presenting as schizoid (Heston 1970; Kallman 1953), (ii) a dominant gene, or (iii) a gene of intermediate nature (Kidd and Cavalli-Storza 1973).
b. A bifactorial theory involving two loci (Karlsson 1966; Matthyssi and Kidd 1976).
c. A polygenic or multifactorial theory (Kidd and Cavalli-Storza 1973). This has two main strands: (i) which does not see schizophrenia as a disease but sees the person as susceptible for many reasons and so incapable of adapting, or at least being extremely sensitive to certain stressors; (ii) which conceptualises schizophrenia as a psychosomatic state (Weiner 1983).
   Both theories (i) and (ii) deny that schizophrenia can be explained in terms of Mendelian genetics, in which MZ (twins) would be 100% concordant.
d. Theories of genetic heterogeneity of Erlenmyer-Kimling (1968), Weiner (1983), which conceptualised schizophrenia as a heterogeneous collection of entities originating from independent and different genetic errors.

We live in a society dominated by what we call the Normalization U-topic Project, in which genetics is particularly prominent in scientific explanations and a particular importance is attached to what is being meant by human behaviour (Rose *et al.* 1984). In 1988 a sensational announcement in the high quality press throughout the world announced triumphantly the discovery of the schizophrenia gene. The details were to be published next in *Nature.* This news item promptly spread to local newspapers and broadcasts. At last many people could be liberated from blame.

The fact is that, as we found, there was then still no agreement from *Nature* to publish the article. Later the article did appear written by Hugh Gurling and his team. The title was 'Localisation of a Susceptibility Locus for Schizophrenia on Chromosome 5' (Sherrington *et al.* 1988). Curiously this article ends in a page of *Nature* where another begins. The latter by Kidd's team was entitled 'Evidence against Linkage of Schizophrenia to Markers on Chromosome 5 in a Northern Swedish Pedigree' (Kennedy *et al.* 1988). Still stranger, *Nature* published in May 1989 a new paper on this subject entitled 'No Linkage of Chromosome 5q 11-q 13 Markers to Schizophrenia in Scottish Families' (Claire *et al.* 1989) confirming Kidd's opinion.

The behaviour of the mass media towards these two last articles was totally different—absolute silence! So the opportunity was lost to redress the idea that psychiatrists and other experts on mental health are trained to hold about schizophrenia and the situation and social status of the schizophrenics, who are perceived too confidently as being carriers, not of an 'alternative psychology' (Cunha-Oliveira 1989) but of a genetic imperfection—a curse.

Parallel to this story another has been spread about some investigations on the so-called manic-depressive psychosis of the Amish population (a religious endogamic sect in the USA.). There was an attempt to study a locus on chromosome 11 (Egeland *et al.* 1987). There were replication studies which did not confirm the earlier thesis (Kelsoe *et al.* 1989). Research in this field is difficult and great caution is required following lessons from the experiences of the history of studies which seem so scientific.

We might, however, cautiously ask—what if one day the genetic cause of schizophrenia is really discovered? Well, for us, it would be a great discovery if it was shown to be the sufficient cause. Even so, as with the transmission of the colour of the eyes and hair texture and colour, which are undoubtedly genetic, what then? Should we one day talk about the 'brown eyes disease'?

In such circumstances, as with the French biologist and geneticist, François Jacob (1970), Nobel Laureate for Medicine and Physiology, we could say: 'it makes no sense to bestow a fraction of the final organisation upon hereditariness and the remaining on ambience, it is the same as asking if Romeo and Juliet's love has a genetic or cultural origin'. We consider the evidence of a genetically sufficient explanation of schizophrenia unlikely and therefore there is something political or projective about the effort put into looking for it as distinct from other factors. In one sense everything in biology depends on laws of susceptibility, tautologically.

The Vulnerability to and Prognosis in Schizophrenia

As the genetics of schizophrenia remain a field for discussion, a false interpretation of heredity can lead to a mythical fatalism and despair. An over-simplified view of the mechanisms and genetic factors in psychiatric disorders can lead to simplistic and undesirable ideas about the diagnosis, therapy and prognosis. Frequently this has bad consequences for the patients, their families and even for society. The preconceptions are a handicap we cannot ignore. It is necessary to point out some of the errors that a simplification of the difference between innate (genetic) and acquired behaviour (environmentally induced) cause. This is an old recurrent error which is still widely occurring at the present time. Transmission of predisposition or tendencies towards schizophrenia are referred to in the psychiatric literature as a vulnerability (that is, a deficiency). Among the several theories of vulnerability we can include the concept of schizotropic fragility presented by Zubin and Spring (1977). It involves the possibility of applying any of the concepts of vulnerability referred to here. This concept, explicitly referring to a predisposition (genetic, environmental or interactive) to develop an abnormal process, has implicit perjorative connotations of undesirable traits and moral stigma.

The word diathesis in contrast to the word vulnerability implies wider possibilities, not least a favourable hereditary predisposition. Vulnerability implies only negative possibilities. For Pieron (1968) the genetic term diathesis implies the capacity (possibility of presenting specific behaviours in certain circumstances having in view the history of the person) and aptitude (which is the substrate of capacity which depends on the degree of maturation or involution, including the education, learning and experience of an individual).

The concept of capacity is virtually free of perjorative connotations and does not imply an increased risk or a vulnerability to schizophrenia, but only implies a probability (that is, a capacity or specific predisposition) to present certain symptoms which are used in the diagnosis of schizophrenia. The genetically transmitted trait might not be abnormal or directly pathogenic. It can only represent a normal (Gaussian variant). In this model the multi-potential traits can lead either to maladjustment or a good adaptation, depending on environmental influences. Karlsson (1970), when studying the relation between creativity and schizophrenia, verified not only that the persons defined as creative had more first-degree relatives diagnosed as schizophrenic, but also that the schizophrenics had more first-degree relatives diagnosed as creative, compared with the normal population.

Among the equivocal views on heredity (for example, the confusion between heredity and congenital diseases, the acceptance of a simple genetic basis for the resemblance between parent and child, and the uncritical acceptance of the heredity of acquired characteristics) we can draw attention to the belief that nothing, or very few things can modify conditions which have a hereditary predisposition. In fact the inherited diseases are not necessarily inevitable nor incurable. Some of them can be prevented or can respond to treatment of modifying environmental factors (for example, diet, exercise, education). It is profoundly mistaken to think that the notion of heredity implies *ipso facto* the notion of chronicity or incurability. It has been on this dangerous and paralysing sophism that the pre-Mendelism concepts of degeneration (B.A. Morel and V. Magnan) and stigma (Morel) and the separation of mental patients as curable and incurable developed in Germany in the nineteenth century. Those concepts had a strong impact on the development of the clinical entity dementia praecox (Kraepelin) and on the damaging way of diagnosing and prognosticating. The prognosis of chronicity is even present in classical works which are widely accepted, for example the textbook of Mayer-Gross, Slater and Roth. In fact the Kraepelinian-Bleulerian-Freudian psychiatry has little place for the recovery of schizophrenics. (E. Bleuler started optimistically and ended up a pessimist, but his son, Manfred, reversed the process.)

Such fatalistic prognosis is contradicted by sufficiently prolonged studies, by several statistical analyses, by the late recoveries, etc. In fact the poor prognoses have been criticised from the beginning of psychiatry and they have been more recently contested and described as the destructive prognosis by H. Baruk. Meninger and Ellenberger also stigmatised bad prognoses as destructive and anti-therapeutic, condemning the patient to self-fulfilling prophecies. As Szasz (1977) says, it would be more correct to attribute the chronicity to certain social expectations (those of the family, the doctor and psychiatrist) and to certain institutional arrangements.

In our opinion, any tendency to consider a human being as a product of genetic determinism risks denying the fact that that person also has an enormous genetically conferred plasticity which confers a great richness and diversity which is so particularly sui generis.

Conclusions

The figures for concordance rates for schizophrenic illnesses are not very different from rates reported for neurotic patients. In the case of anxiety neurosis, for example, Slater and Shields (1969) found a concordance rate of 65% for MZ twins and 13% for DZ twins. As regards obsessional neurosis, Carey (1978) has reported a study of a consecutive series of twin probands with obsessional neurosis presenting to the Maudsley Hospital. Six of the twelve MZ co-twins had had treatment for nervous complaints—three had definite and a further two had possible obsessional features. Only one of the twelve DZ co-twins was obsessional. McGuffin and Mawson (1980) have also described two pairs of MZ twins concordant for obsessional neurosis; in each pair the proband and co-twin developed their symptoms independently and without prior knowledge of the other's illness—despite this fact there was a marked similarity of symptoms within each pair.

These findings remind us of the research strategy that has used MZ twins who have been brought up apart with the aim of teasing out more clearly the role of genetic and environmental factors in schizophrenia. In fact, if we find a remarkable concordance rate in a given group of MZ twins with regard to the clinical diagnosis of schizophrenia, we have first to overcome the objection that the similarities may result from a similar environment before we can be sure that they are due to hereditary factors. This was also one of the most obvious flaws of the pioneer family studies carried out by authors like Rudin or Kallmann. The study of monozygotic twins separated at a very early age and brought up apart can help to solve this problem, in conjunction with the study of adopted-away offsprings of schizophrenic parents.

The known number of MZ twins reared apart and concordance for schizophrenia is, on the whole, bigger than the known number of MZ pairs living apart and discordant for this mental disorder (Kringlen 1967). For the time being, however, we only know a few cases fulfilling all these requirements and cannot therefore draw any definite conclusions. On the other hand, we must not forget that twin pairs are not infrequently reported (or chosen for research and publication) precisely because they are concordant for schizophrenia; in systematically collected series discordant pairs seem to be more usual.

A detailed examination of these case histories (MZ twin pairs reared apart and concordant for schizophrenia) shows, moreover, that most twin pairs, although reared apart in different physical environments, were in fact subjected to very similar socio-cultural and emotional conditions—many of them grew up in orphanages or were raised by relatives of their biological parents, in equally unsatisfactory socio-economic backgrounds.

It seems, therefore, that the researchers who first studied MZ twins reared apart were rather uncritical in accepting their findings as undeniable proof of the decisive significance of heredity in the aetiology of schizophrenia. In our opinion, we would be entitled to ascribe a significant aetiological role to genetic factors only if we could find concordant MZ twin pairs that had been separated in early childhood and raised in quite different (but emotionally sound) family conditions. Also, concordance between siblings of schizophrenic parents must be significantly higher than that between siblings of normal parents when they have all been adopted when very young and reared in emotionally stable environments. To avoid obstetric problems some studies need to show positive results studying siblings only from schizophrenic and normal fathers. Further, it is necessary that the results should be similar for siblings from mothers and fathers. There should be significant differences between experimental and control groups in three categories—the siblings from fathers, from father and mother, and between the parents of the control and experimental group.

Having in view the inconclusive evidence provided so far by the best designed studies with regard to the role of heredity in schizophrenia, and taking into account the fact that similar findings have been obtained in the case of psychodynamically understandable mental disorders (such as anxiety neurosis and obsessional neurosis), we think it is reasonable to regard (at least for the time being) the genetic basis of schizophrenia as a relatively weak and non-specific polygenic disposition, allowing for a considerable (and in the end much more relevant from a heuristic viewpoint) environmental influence—as, for instance, in the case of neurotic patients.

In this connection, it seems appropriate to quote Kringlen (1967):

> There are, however, no schizophrenic or for that matter neurotic genes... I do not think that the environmental factors operate as a release mechanism for schizophrenia; more likely, schizophrenic development has to be looked upon as the result of a combination of endogenous and exogenous factors, a developmental interaction... The study of schizophrenia must be linked to the study of normal personality development. The solution of the so-called schizophrenia riddle will, generally speaking, not come from any simple biochemical 'breakthrough' since there are no simple biochemical answers to variations in intelligence, height and weight, blood pressure, epileptic disposition. Part of the solution may well be found in the near future, possibly through meticulous research in the field of social science. Here then lie our hopes—which are not great—for a social prevention.

Chapter 8

A New Paradigm for Schizophrenia?

The scientific mentality because it thinks in a causal way is unable to think ahead. It only understands the past. So this knowledge can only capture half of the soul.

C.G. Jung

IN THIS chapter we will present the idiographic approach to schizophrenic patients' behaviour, and also to the writing of biography as a means of understanding their acts and experiences. This implies that schizophrenia is more akin to some varieties of life processes than to a specific kind of disease. As Bleuler (1978) put it:

> According to our present-day concept, schizophrenics flounder under the same difficulties with which all of us struggle all our lives. In spite of our own inner discords, or ambivalences, and our ambitendencies, all of us must find ways and means for establishing an awareness of our own 'egos' and for confronting the world with our own wills. As long as we recognise in the schizophrenic a fellow sufferer and comrade-in-arms, he remains one of us. But when we see in him someone whom a pathological heritage or a degenerate brain has rendered inaccessible, inhuman, different or strange, we involuntarily turn away from him. Yet it is so very beneficial to the schizophrenic for us to stay close to him! (cf. Hare 1979).

In another passage of the same book, Bleuler called our attention to the fact that,

> even in healthy people there is some disposition in the direction of schizophrenic psychic life and that such disposition might perhaps be a normal part of human nature. This indeed has been proved by research into the psychology of the healthy; beneath the surface of healthy psychic life enabling us to adapt to others and to the real world there is hidden in every man a chaotic inner life which goes on without consideration of reality. This chaotic and illogical inner life cannot be distinguished from the schizophrenic way of thinking, imagining and living. Perhaps we may conclude: the symptomatology of schizophrenic psychoses is not always the same resulting from a common cause, but is always of the same type, because schizophrenic disease reveals the same human tendencies.

We disagree, however, with some of the concepts put forward by Bleuler in this passage of his book; for instance, his emphasis on the chaotic and illogical features of schizophrenic patients' inner life, as if for him this inner life were inexplicable and had nothing to do with patients' actual life experiences.

Ciompi (1980: 420), after describing in detail his huge follow-up study of 1,642 schizophrenic patients (selected from a catchment area of about 500,000 inhabitants and studied during an average period of 36.9 years), concluded his paper with the following comments:

> For everybody who does not link the concept of schizophrenia itself to an obligatory bad outcome, the enormous variety of possible evolutions shows that there is no such thing as a specific course of schizophrenia. Doubtless the potential for improvement of schizophrenia has for a long time been grossly under-estimated. In the light of long-term investigations, what is called the course of schizophrenia more closely resembles a life process open to a great variety of influences of all kinds than an illness with a given course. Just as in normal life processes, here what we call illness may represent the complex and variable reaction to an equally complex global situation of a given person, with his particular sensibilities and idiosyncrasies, personality structure, behaviour and communication patterns, and past and present experiences... Practically none of the old and seemingly secure dogmas about this illness hold when we look at them closely and long enough. But also no approach which takes the person into account more than the illness, and is hence 'psychotherapeutic' in a wider or narrower sense, has to be a priori discarded. Viewing schizophrenia as closer to a life process than to an illness might not be a less useful concept for therapeutic purposes than any other. Anyhow it inspires hope as well as modesty in dealing and communicating with our fellow men hidden by the fascinating and as yet unsolved enigma of psychotic alienation.

It is interesting to compare Ciompi's follow-up study with the strategy chosen by Huber (1983) for his own research project. In fact, this German author, contrary to Ciompi's approach, decided to emphasise the pathological nature of schizophrenia and followed his patients in terms of psychopathological symptoms and types of remission, such as complete remission, pure residual syndromes, structural deformity without psychosis, mixed residues, typically schizophrenic defect psychosis, chronic pure psychosis and structural deformity with psychosis. (Language is really a very seductive tool but often it confuses more than clarifies the issues at stake.)

The decision we have taken to study schizophrenics' experience and behaviour as if they were legitimate varieties of life process forces us to confront the problem of patients' responsibility regarding the design and unfolding of their relation with the world and fellow men.

If we view these human beings not as passive victims of a complex of morbid factors but as active protagonists of their history and destiny, we find ourselves more inclined to discuss with them the role played by their personal responsibility vis-à-vis not only their past (and present) misery but also the making of their future life.

We are only too aware that their situation is a disturbed and undesirable one and that we cannot handle the burden of personal responsibility as we are entitled to do in the case of a sound mind. Nevertheless, we think that if the role of each patient's responsibility is acknowledged as a part of the causal equation, our attitude towards the clinical interaction (and also towards what we will then consider to be correct therapy) will be more meaningful and sensible (Frankl 1963; Frankl 1978; Furlong 1981).

This way of thinking about patients' own participation in the incubation, emergence and course of their psychotic illnesses implies that we will approach in a different frame of mind the planning of our clinical interventions, such as diagnosis and treatment. If we vote for this style of doctor-patient relationship we will have to take into account the effect of patients' choices, decisions, projections and value-judgments upon their careers as mentally abnormal people (Margulies and Havens 1981).

In this new light the clinical dialogue appears nearer to a process of negotiation between human beings than to a ritual of detached clinical observation. Negotiation necessarily implies compromise and the disclosure of doctors' personal world-views, which they hope will help patients to overcome and modify their undesirable situation.

Patients are often confused about life. They can become anxious and frightened (or aggressive to others and/or themselves) and sometimes we have no other alternative than to resort to drugs or other drastic methods of physical restraint. However, if we decide to ascribe a role to patients' responsibility and ultimate humanness, we will be more willing to regard this kind of pharmacological trick as a secondary component of a wider strategy of action, whose nucleus consists of a meaningful dialogue based on the human potential of both doctor and patient. Greben (1981: 453) wrote in this connection:

> The therapist must in some ways address himself to destructive, constricting or self-defeating behaviour. He must somehow stand on the side of constructive and effective living on the part of the patient. To say that the therapist must not reveal his position on such matters is foolish. Can the therapist not enter into the fact that the patient is depressed, or suicidal, or homicidal, or a thief, or a hermit? Can he not let his feelings be known about the patient's use of drugs, or avoidance of work, or repeated involvement with destructive partners? Of course not...The excessively or deceptively passive therapist may choose not to show such leanings, but many of them will be known to the patient nonetheless. When a non-interventionist position is taken too far, endless therapy can occur without effect; many of the failures of psychotherapy can be attributed to the fact that therapists have worked in this misguided way (Greben and Lesser 1976).

'Men are doomed to be free', as Sartre (1943) has said, and in the case of schizophrenia nothing has proved that personal freedom and responsibility are concepts alien to the nature of 'his disturbed (and disturbing) condition' (McGlashan and Carpenter 1981). Perhaps psychosis and schizophrenia are prices men must pay for being thrown into a world where they have to find (and make) their way without the help of any concrete set of norms, valid for all times and places.

Freedom brings with it the need for personal choices and decisions, as well as inevitable doubts and conflicts, frustrations and defeats. As Merleau-Ponty (1945) put it:

> Even what are called obstacles to freedom are in reality deployed by it. An unclimbable rock face, a large or small, vertical or slanting rock, are things which have no meaning for anyone who is not intending to surmount them, for a subject whose projects do not carve out such determinate forms from the uniform mass of the 'in itself' and cause an orientated world to arise—a significance in things. There is, then, ultimately nothing that can set limits to freedom, except those limits that freedom itself has set in the form of its various initiatives, so that the subject has simply the external world that he gives himself. Since it is the latter who, on coming into being, brings to light significance and value in things, and since nothing can impinge upon it except through acquiring, thanks to it, significance and value, there is no action of things on the subject but merely a signification (in the active sense), a centrifugal *Sinngebung*.

For some people these are challenges, for which no 'ego defence mechanisms' seem to be effective enough (Scharfetter 1981). This human yearning for safety and purpose in life, for hard and fast rules of conduct, is well depicted by the Spanish philosopher, Ortega y Gasset (1957) when he writes:

> Take stock of those around you and you will hear them talking in precise terms about themselves and their surroundings, which would seem to point to them having ideas on the matter. But start to analyse those ideas and you will find that they hardly reflect in any way the reality to which they appear to refer, and if you go deeper you will discover that there is not even an attempt to adjust the ideas to this reality. Quite the contrary, through these notions the individual is trying to cut off any personal vision of reality, of his own very life. For life is at the start a chaos in which one is lost. The individual suspects this but he is frightened at finding himself face to face with this terrible reality and tries to cover it up with a curtain of fantasy, where everything is clear. It does not worry him that his 'ideas' are not true, he uses them as trenches for the defence of his existence, as scarecrows to frighten away reality.

We suspect something very similar also happens (although in a much more extreme and distorted way) in the case of those unfortunate people whose undesirable life processes we usually identify by means of the label schizophrenia.

The Psychiatrist's Human Potential and the Treatment of Schizophrenia

Here we endeavour to demonstrate that schizophrenic patients, although sensitive and mistaken people, can become less disturbed and suspicious by grasping that they are also able to act and think as responsible and socially effective people who have still time left to make some sense of their lives. As Laing (1978) wrote: 'In this sense, therefore, the task in psychotherapy was to make, using Jaspers's expression, an appeal to the freedom of the patient. A good deal of the skill in psychotherapy lies in the ability to do this effectively'.

Nevertheless, though we are inclined to conclude that classical psychiatry has underrated psychiatrists' (and patients') humanistic capacity, we think there are good grounds to stress the complexity of the undertaking. Psychiatry is about people and particularly in the case of schizophrenia we are bound to deal with very intricate human problems and relationships demanding a heavy commitment from mental health professionals.

This kind of commitment implies new responsibilities for psychiatrists since it requires one not to be content with physical treatments and sedation, as that possibly only obscures the problem or allows the truth to be avoided. The task is difficult and risky, and one can disturb a hornet's nest. In addition to this, our job must be performed in the middle of ideological battles within psychiatry, involving for instance neurophysiology and psychodynamics, biochemistry and social work, as well as civil liberties agencies, patients' neighbours, relatives and friends, nursing unions, police and judges (Dell 1980).

We see, therefore, how a discussion concerning the role of psychiatrists' human potential in the treatment of schizophrenia calls forth not only the necessary concern for patients' personal responsibility and capacity for self-improvement but also the wide range of difficulties brought about by the practice of a profession whose most distinctive aim is to deal with the hazardous business of human relationships in a problematic social, cultural, historical and institutional context (Goffman 1980; Sullivan 1931).

The Emergence of a New Paradigm for Schizophrenia

From what we have said about the 'facts' that have been brought about by research on schizophrenia, we conclude that the evidence gathered does not warrant our viewing schizophrenia as an incomprehensible psychotic process having nothing to do with schizophrenic patients' world-views, biographies and attitudes to life and fellowmen. This tendency to conceptualise schizophrenia in terms of an extreme contrast with normal behaviour is the expression of the paradigms more or less deliberately applied by many psychiatrists to the interpretation of their patients' undesirable experiences and behaviour.

As Kuhn (1970) wrote:

> Given a paradigm, interpretation of data is central to the enterprise that explores it. But that interpretative enterprise can only articulate a paradigm, not correct it. Paradigms are not corrigible by normal science at all. Instead, as we have already seen, normal science ultimately leads only to the recognition of anomalies and crises. And these are terminated, not by deliberation and interpretation, but by a relatively sudden and unstructured event like the Gestalt switch...What chemists took from Dalton was not new experimental laws but a new way of practising chemistry (he himself called it the 'new system of chemical philosophy'), and this proved so rapidly fruitful that only a few of the older chemists in France and Britain were able to resist it. As a result, chemists came to live in a world where reactions behaved quite differently from the way they had before.

It was with the aim of underlining the anomalies that have been revealed, as regards the nature of schizophrenia, by what Kuhn calls normal science, that we decided to approach (and interact with) schizophrenic patients in the assumption that they are understandable people with whom we can have a meaningful dialogue. We hope this new way of looking at our patients' predicament (which so far has not been proved wrong by any kind of overwhelming evidence) will contribute to the appearance of different and more useful paradigms, and consequently to more sensible styles of practising psychiatry.

As Kuhn (1970: 122) puts it in the same book:

> During scientific revolutions scientists see new and different things when looking with familiar instruments in places they have looked before. It is rather as if the professional community had been suddenly transported to another planet where familiar objects are seen in a different light and are joined by unfamiliar ones as well.

Can a belief in the possibility of (more or less incompletely) understanding schizophrenic patients and making sense of their behaviour and experiences lead to our professional community being transported to another planet where familiar objects are seen in a different light? We think there are reasons to try this experiment, even though the weight of certain past successes

(G.P.I. treatment for instance) still provides psychiatrists with powerful alibis for not doing so. Kuhn addressed himself to this same problem when he wrote:

> Many readers will surely want to say that what changes with a paradigm is only the scientist's interpretation of observations that themselves are fixed by the nature of the environment and of the perceptual apparatus. On this view, Priestly and Lavoisier both saw oxygen, but they interpreted their observations differently. Aristotle and Galileo both saw pendulums but they differed in their interpretations of what they both had seen. Let me say at once that this very usual view of what occurs when scientists change their minds about fundamental matters can be neither all wrong nor a mere mistake. Rather it is an essential part of a philosophical paradigm initiated by Descartes and developed at the same time as Newtonian dynamics. That paradigm has served both science and philosophy well. Its exploitation, like that of dynamics itself, has been fruitful of a fundamental understanding that perhaps could not have been achieved in another way. But, as the example of Newtonian dynamics also indicates, even the most striking past successes provide no guarantee that crisis can be indefinitely postponed.

Because we do not wish to postpone indefinitely a better understanding of the lives and actions of those disturbed (and disturbing) people we call schizophrenics, we decided to test a new paradigm and see how it would work in the context of our daily psychiatric praxis.

Conclusions

The view that schizophrenia is a disease of civilisations has begun to elicit interest in the light of work in cultural and anthropological fields. This is hardly surprising if, with M. de la Palice, we see schizophrenia as a neologism inserted into professional jargon by Eugene Bleuler, who did so thinking it had been previously overlooked. This led to a belief that certain collections of undesirable symptoms were aspects of an entity, indeed a clinical disease. For schizophrenia this was accepted without discussion. Gaston (1978) referred in fact to 'Schneider's (1972) postulate "that the affective disorders and schizophrenia are symptoms of unknown diseases"'. However, as we hope we have demonstrated, such opinions still await substantiation. Yet it is upon such concepts that psychiatry has based itself. They are enshrined in Jaspers's depiction of a *Prozess*. That describes the onset of madness as an unpredictable event, independent of the life story and the meaning of events in it.

We have been struck recently by the similarity between the experiences of schizophrenia, creativity, being enamoured of something or somebody, and feeling inspired by the sacred. We put these states together under the rubric of nascent states in the sense of Alberoni (1983). Baczko (1985) sees society as having utopian plans, but that is what we see as subverted by the nascent states. Hence the attempt is made to domesticate, neutralise and institutionalise them in the church, marriage and asylums. Alberoni (1983) questions the origins of such common ideas, as for example seeing being enamoured as an egotistical and inward-looking idea. His answer is that it is from the political, ideological and religious institutions which pretend to have a total control of the individuals. Clearly the nascent states disrupt any power based on rationality. As the Bible puts it:

> Suppose ye that I am come to give peace on earth?
> I tell you, Nay; but rather division:
> For from henceforth there shall be five in one house divided, three against two,
> and two against three.
> The father shall be divided against the son, and the son against the father; the
> mother against the daughter,
> and the daughter against the mother; the mother in law against her daughter in
> law, and the daughter in law against her mother in law.

Although the nascent states seem extraordinary, they all arise from being human. They involve a new type of vertigo-like state in which the individual has to struggle to be a in a world separated from causality and everyday meanings. This world is described by von Gebsattel (1954) as the world of the marvellous. The nascent states are characteristics of ordinary men and women and do not depend on something extra-terrestrial. If they call into question the stability and routines of institutions, this is also because the institutions cannot and do not want by definition to conspire against themselves in the light of the uncertainties of the human condition they exist to control and regulate.

The confrontation between the subversive power of the nascent states and of the state itself and its institutions has been referred to by Franca Ongaro Basaglia (1982: 132) as follows:

> The danger, the menace, is in human nature; it is especially so in certain people in whom unreason is personified. Then it is enough to identify and isolate them before they produce the contagion and before they destroy the rational order. The identification and isolation is achieved in a differentiated way according to the quality and kind of apopheny (revelation) and its contagiousness and power to succeed. To illustrate this conceptualisation we can consider the power of the contagion of the psychological experiences of St Paul and the revelations to the Prophet Mohamed.
>
> In the concrete case of schizophrenia (the most individual and least contagious Nascent State), the power utilised or the mechanism of control is that of

> *diminutio capitis* (reduced responsibility). By schizophrenia we mean that apopheny which is so personal that it cannot easily be shared. An apopheny widely enough shared leaves the field of psychiatry. The schizophrenics are said to have a disease. This conceptualisation is only a caricature of the ordinary mental concept. It has only those features or symptoms because of which Schneider called it an organic state! This concept of disease only survives because of the extrapolations that are made from the pharmacological effects of certain soporific drugs. What seems to be happening is what Chartier (1988) calls mere legitimation of a certain discipline of power by institutional recognition by that same power of what can be considered as a science.
>
> It is by acting according to a regulatory code[1] that psychiatrists legitimate themselves as scientific. The prestige of science among laymen in a desacredised society, which has lost the transcendental, the marvellous, the extraordinary, justifies the power which without this prestige would be arbitrary and discriminatory. The function of the science is to show that the defect is in the individual (genetically or otherwise) but not in the social norm. It is within this code, which only the psychiatrist understands, that the schizophrenic enmeshes himself ever more completely. Recently a so-called schizophrenic said: 'Doctor, psychiatry has many symptoms but my problem is nervousness'.

Frank Kafka (1935) presented a similarly absurd situation of a trial in which the legal process is unknown. The denouncer can be anyone, any citizen or accomplice of the status quo but in it only the accused becomes notorious. Becoming increasingly notorious he loses more and more of his humanity. In the trial of Joseph K. the friendly warder says:

> 'What do you want? Do you think you can accelerate your beautiful trial only because you are blaming us?'...We are only simple subordinates...We have nothing to do with you only oversee you ten hours a day. For this we are paid. This is all we are, but we understand perfectly that the leaders for whom we work before giving us such responsibility must be adequately informed of the reasons for the detention and about the person detained...this is the law so how can it be mistaken?,
>
> 'I don't know this law' answered K...'it probably does not exist'.
>
> 'Look Wilhelm, he says he doesn't know the law although he declares himself innocent.'
>
> 'You are right Franz, but you will never find a man like this who grasps the reasons involved.'

The guilt resided in his being different from others. That is because he tries to be himself and not anyone else. So his guilt increases with his trial, which reveals, isolates and annihilates him while normality (the law) remains

1. See, for example, the Diagnostic and Statistical Manual of the American Psychiatric Association (DSM.III).

ill-defined and damaging. Individuals when isolated by a trial reveal themselves as deviating from the normality which does not exist. In the trial against Joseph K. the inspector said: 'You might be advisedly more reserved since what you have just said can influence the assessment of your behaviour. The right word here and there would be in your interest'. The trial continued its inexorable course to the chronicity of ***diminutio capitis***, that is to that defect state of the social standing of the individual. In fact to his annihilation.

Of normality (a law) we only know what Barthes (1981: 44) said:

> Everyone imposes his own *system of being*...to be 'normal' ('without love') it would be necessary for me to find Coluche amusing, the restaurant good, the painting beautiful, and the Corpus Christi feast animated...it is not only to tolerate power but also to sympathise with it.

Every citizen lives in the context of this law called normality, presupposing that he will never transcend the limits of anonymous mediocrity. If he does overstep this limit he can be taken not to the courts of justice but to a Kafkaesque trial.

The process is not judicial but a clinical trial. It is not regulated by a law of the state but by a law of science. As Szasz wrote (1970):

> Medicine replaces theology, the alienist replaced the inquisitors, and the mental patients replaced the witches. As a result mass religious movements are replaced by mass medical movements. So the persecution of heretics was replaced by persecution of mental patients.

In Portugal the first trial of a 'nascent state' of Aberoni was in the fourteenth century with the barbaric execution of Da Ines de Castro (1355) for the 'crime' of being in love with D Pero I (King of Portugal). The king (who was married to Da Constans Manuel) responded by making all the courtiers kiss the dead hand of Da Ines de Castro, whom the king called the queen. The case brings into focus the conflict between reason and passion, since by the end of the Middle Ages it is the rationalisation of power which has increased. This was particularly exemplified by the triumph of the French Revolution (1789–1799). One of the other most powerful triumphs of nationality was the Inquisitor. This achieved the aim of destroying human differences (to be Jewish, Islamic, a heretic or a witch). With the French Revolution though, there emerged the first founders of psychiatry and the beginning of the modern state, which brought about the marginalisation of the popular (cf. Jenner and Kendall 1991).

In psychiatry and particularly for the schizophrenic, the Kafkaesque process begins the moment someone detects in another the eruption of a Jasperian *Prozess*.[1] To put it another way, it starts the moment the nascent

1. It is of some interest to note that *Prozess* in the German of Kafka and *Processo* in

state of Alberoni or the *ganz andere* de Eliade (1952) commences. As Chartier (1988: 17) wrote: 'Although modern politics are influenced by old traditions and symbols, they are primarily the *prescription of the popular*'.

The similarity of the views of those who have concerned themselves with nascent states (and clearly we include schizophrenia among them) cannot fail to impress us. For Alberoni (1983) for example, 'falling in love is a revolution. The more complex, articulated and rich the new order is, the more terrible is the *development*, the more difficult, dangerous and risky is the *process*'. So, perhaps it is easier to understand why Schneider (1972) permitted himself the sibilline statement that 'the goal of a completely somatological resolution of the psychiatry of psychoses is infinitely, incalculably distant'.

The same infinite, incalculable distance is the one which exists between a work of art, for instance, and the contingent clinical history of its creator. There is in fact a sea of humanity which overflows the timid bounds of reason. In the words of Teixeira de Pascoaes (1984): 'Man is the only animal who does not coincide with the world; his destiny is to expand the world to match the scope of his imagination'.

If today reason holds power exclusively, we understand the way it exercises its tyranny over unreason, accusing it, putting it on trial under the darkest of suspicions. And the worst suspicion is to suppose that unreason is of non-human origin or—which comes to the same thing—is altogether unworthy of the category human. It is thus necessarily supposed to be an historico-anthropological atavism, a genetic error, a virus infection (aggression), a biochemical fault, etc. Even the authors of this book, simply because they question the ontology of the existence of a clinical entity called schizophrenia, but do not deny the need to help some people called schizophrenics, do not escape the suspicion of being carriers of a bad gene, of being members of some magico-esoteric sect, or of having been infected by the crow virus. Recently, Hare (1988) admitted enormous difficulty in detecting the presence of schizophrenia before the nineteenth century. He does not realise nevertheless that to look for schizophrenia before Kraepelin-Jaspers-Bleuler constituted it (put it together) would be as useless as to look for transgressions of the Napoleonic Code before it was instituted (compiled) (1804). In our view it would have been very surprising if Hare had managed to find, outside the nineteenth and twentieth centuries, the most specific consequences of the predominant socio-cultural conditions in the last

the Portuguese, from which this translation was made, have three meanings. In English process has two meanings; they are the processes of everyday English and that of Karl Jaspers. However, for a third meaning in English, process has to be translated as trial in the legal sense, so English loses some of the play on words in the two original languages.

two centuries in the so-called Western World; the systematic eradication of the unforeseeable, the spontaneous and the irrational. Thus the crow virus is a close relative of the one which purports to (might) explain transgressions of criminal and civil law from the nineteenth century onward.

Certainly we consider that all nascent states have in common a great potential for disorder, for chaos incompatible with the maintenance and stability of the modern state. Dante (1921) wrote: 'I thought that the universe felt love, through which some believe the world often returns to chaos'. Certainly we also consider that all these nascent states release conflict and instability, particularisms and the unforeseeable circumstances. All that is what central power's role is, to dominate and regulate. For Castel: 'If local politico-administrative bodies were self-regulating, it would lead to penury, shortage of resources, inability to dominate and regulate conflicts and the risk of the appearance, at a local level, of new feudalities and new particularisms'. We might ask what is this great risk after all? For the only damage is to central power itself and its myths: national history, official language, obligatory schooling, psychiatry. Where penury and shortage of resources are concerned, it is worth noting that it is the small European states, vestiges of feudalities that have the higher standard of living: Holland, Belgium, Switzerland, Luxembourg, Lichtenstein and Monaco and Andorra.

Clearly the problem which arises here is that of chaos versus structure, of what is unstructured as opposed to what is structured. Curiously this problem is one which is posed only in so-called Western society, and does not make any sense in other types of society of the sort our culture tends to call 'third world' and 'primitive', where so-called traditional norms (models) predominate.

If the role of the modern state power is to impose a rational structure on communities in which the traditional unstructuredness is always latent, then it has need of a legitimacy which previously derived from a universal and state religion. With power going into the hands of laity, the place of this religion was taken by what is understood as science, and in this sense scientific knowledge begins to legitimize the requirements of power, and so to dominate and regulate the so-called conflicts.

For psychiatrists it is particularly important to understand which conflicts we are encharged by power to dominate and regulate—small rational conflicts and those which are determined by nascent states. This is the object of psychiatric biochemistry, genetics and biostatistics.

The dominance of the genetics and biochemistry of human beings accused of being ill can only lead to an identikit society (look-alikes)—inhuman, cold, without conflicts, without emotions, without greatness. That is to paraphrase Dodds (1988), a place where everything is so terribly rational.

What then is our paradigm? Simply a view that human beings live with tensions between their own and other people's needs. They live in a world about which they cannot have ontological confidence. One, though, in which to be called normal often requires common-sense responses to the concepts of time, space, God, freedom, self, morals, responsibility and matter. It is certainly dangerous in many circumstances to dwell on these issues, especially to make them really matters of central concern. It is safer to see them as irrelevant to the real problems of living.

To some extent the historical period gives an outline of what it is wise to seem to accept. In the mediaeval period God, the Father, was in heaven and each had his feudal place, as in the Hindu castes. Now capitalism and science explain what must be. Individuals in each system have however had problems with it. They do not like to believe there can be no alternative.

In a very successful ideology of our period, matter as atoms recurrently colliding had the innate ability subsequently to perceive itself aesthetically. The epiphenomenological dualist or monist dilemmas for neo-Darwinism presented by that apparent fact of the thoughtless universe developing thinking might seem stupid to contemplate. The success of the sciences has too obviously depended on asking questions which can be answered, pushing the imponderables on one side. Living, however, demands practical responses with insufficient guidelines, and for many their security lies in beliefs. The questions posed by life are the inevitable issues for the human being's existence and values, not just the convenient ones to answer to further careers and acceptability. Yet it is wise to take that into account too. Technology, though, has to be evaluated. Some facts are trivial even if publishable in learned journals, which conveniently emphasise the impossibility of knowing what a piece of research will lead to. But there is something very inauthentic and stilted about the person who actually technicalises life and sees values as meaningless or absolute. Are his relationships to be treated similarly? Such persons are usually frightened of the other, more so even than most of us.

Looking at the starry sky with Kant and wondering about it and our minds must not preoccupy us. We must make breakfast etc., but man does not live by bread alone. To be secure, though, much must be under control. Trying to explain everything obscures the mysteries behind things and leads one to exclude the disruptive person who would damage the security achieved by having put things into some sort of order.

Individuals require power through knowledge within this strange Kafkaesque system. However, they have been produced by the system and their language and morality, indeed their world, is a social product. Their childhood taught them their need of love and of other people; it showed that good (that is, complicit) children are rewarded. Much becomes concretised conceptually and the firm beliefs of common sense are embedded or introjected. Strange ideas tend to develop when beliefs begin to fail, when integration is not rewarded, when one is socially and personally stranded and alone in the strange world, and perhaps angry and hurt. The attempt to go it alone can then lead to a spiral of rejection, to isolation, to false perceptions and/or experiences, and segregation and diagnosis. Worse still one cannot escape. There is nowhere to get away from the social nexus and reality in which one's emotions are so intimately and inevitably enmeshed. Geography is irrelevant, indeed physical separation makes the heart grow fonder and sometimes more angry.

The formidable task of being alone and struggling to produce a new language with which to speak to nobody and yet to blame everybody else for one's own discomfort produces unbearable tensions. One wishes to be very special but one is not. In order to be secure, core constructs are tenaciously, almost randomly, sought and maintained. What is face-saving in one's own mind, which is damaging to one's image in others, seems essential. Vascillation and thrashing around in a rough sea, grabbing hold of this or that plank (of belief in their language) in order to survive and breathe freely, follows. Everything makes everything worse, especially those who think they are helping.

I am! Yet what I am who cares, or knows?
My friends forsake me like a memory lost.
I am the self-consumer of my woes;
They rise and vanish, an oblivious host,
Shadows of life, whose very soul is lost.
And yet I am—I live—though I am toss'd
Into the nothingness of scorn and noise,
Into the living sea of waking dream,
Where there is neither sense of life, nor joys,
But the huge shipwreck of my own esteem
And all that's dear. Even those I loved the best
Are strange—nay, they are stranger than the rest.
I long for scenes where man has never trod—
For scenes where a woman never smiled or wept—
There to abide with my Creator, God,
And sleep as I in childhood sweetly slept,
Full of high thoughts, unborn. So let me lie—
The grass below; above, the vaulted sky.

JOHN CLARE 1793–1864

Perhaps our paradigm is that people in that sort of state of mind are so difficult to live with. They suffer and they are also insufferable, and so are called schizophrenics by those society has ordained to do so.

Perhaps we can return to Pessoa:

> In reality the unique critics of art and literature ought to be the psychiatrists; although they are as ignorant about the issues and as remote from them, and about what they call science as other people, nevertheless when faced with mental disease they have the competence that our judgment says they have. No body of human knowledge can be built on any other bases.

What must we do then? We suggest we could continue to try to accept and understand them, however hard it is. It is hard and alone is not effective, the possibility of rejoining us and the advantages of at least some complicity, which does not produce overwhelming fear and guilt, must become apparent to them. Then perhaps something more congenial can be erected in their lives, with us and ours. So it seems to us, but we too may be very mistaken.

APPENDIX

1947-1987 ANTONIO CARLOS DAVIM DA SILVA MONTEIRO

It seems fitting to conclude with a tribute to Antonio Carlos Monteiro, in whose company many of the insights in this book developed. Perhaps in world and historical terms forty is not so young to die, but Antonio Carlos Monteiro was to our minds both young and a man with great promise. When he came to Sheffield (1979-1983) I felt that I had been entrusted with one of Portugal's finer sons. He also seemed to display to me a much undeserved filial piety. He did on first impression present as a formal, slightly pedantic, aristocratic and courteous Portuguese gentleman, meticulous in his dress and behaviour. Such superficial appearances were quickly dispelled when he presented himself as a libertine Frenchman at a fancy dress party, and was accompanied by his wife and accomplice who was dressed up as his over-ornamented Parisian companion. Their contribution to the fun also involved expert lessons for all in elegant leadership of the Samba.

Antonio knew a lot about the good things of life; he was a missionary among the Anglo-Saxons whom he saw lacked imagination, especially in culinary arts. His knowledge of all sports, especially football, was encyclopaedic and he was slightly unbearable when Portugal beat England in the World Cup qualifying round. In a chauvinistic frame of mind, I told him we were just encouraging them. When in fact, unlike us, they failed to qualify for the next round, he wrote thanking me but warning us not to take such generous risks in the future as they would not work!

There was a great love of Portugal in Antonio's soul. We were all encouraged to read Luis de Camões and to compare him with Shakespeare. In addition, after Christmas when we went to see English folk-dancing in the local streets, he compared it a little unfavourably with the Fado. He revealed his psychodynamics, of which he was intensely aware, by, as a *non sequitur*, suddenly explaining that Portuguese sailors discovered Japan when their population was the same size as that of Sheffield. He waxed eloquent on the Portuguese ending the death sentence before any other European country and rightly receiving praise from Voltaire. He had had plenty of Port and Vinho Verde, which he had imported for us, not unmixed with English beer at the time.

Antonio's love of his homeland was, however, quite outstripped by his warmth to all people and both loves were able to interact at their best when one visited him and Dina in Porto. Nobody was more hospitable; everything was presented, Portugal's finest treasures, wines and restaurants, and some of its social problems too.

Naturally, mentioning love one must mention Dina (Constantina) Golfi, Antonio's Greek wife. Both were involved in his work and both were very devoted to each other. Both were impressive polyglots and she, while a liberated feminist in one sense, was willing to give up her career in law for him. I realised that she loved psychiatry too; she also particularly liked the meals we had with the patients.

I started this appendix attempting a pen portrait of someone whom, as one of my postgraduate students, I learnt to admire and love. Our world seemed shattered when we knew that Antonio was doomed. The poignancy of his courage and good humour through trying periods of very toxic medication, of blood transfusions, a splenectomy, tiredness due to anaemia, as well as pain, added to our respect. The night before he died, when he was connected up to several tubes, I sat for a too short while by his bed and his last words to me were expressed with a dry mouth: 'I am not on good form tonight'. Dina and her father had been at the bedside for days.

Most of my conversations with Antonio and the raison d'etre for our coming together concerned schizophrenia. He was at first very cautious about this English professor he had once chauffered to yet another beanfeast in Porto. Perhaps he thought I was a stereotyped classical psychiatrist who expected regimental discipline of even the younger people's thoughts. I like to believe that he had, until he came to Sheffield, only been dimly aware of a much more existentially-based approach.

Antonio learnt how to disagree with me without causing offence. One area in particular involved the chaotic sexuality of the psychotic. He saw the psychosis as primary, I the sexuality, but we both agreed about the importance of learning to know the person himself rather than the patient and psychopathology. Antonio's PhD thesis 'The Concepts of Understanding and the Schizophrenia Problem' was based on that, as is illustrated by our joint chapter in this book on Jaspers's concept of understanding.

One particularly disturbed 'schizophrenic' sticks in my mind. He was violent to other patients and the staff and was acting like an animal. He was so frightening that everyone, like me, tightened controls on him and locked him in a room, where he took off his clothes and received more medication. Antonio implied that my madness and fears were as great as the patient's; he needed at that very stage to be allowed to go home. I trembled at the thought but somehow, hours later, decided with great nervousness to risk it. The 'animal' dressed himself, looked quite smart and returned home to his wife and children, who reported that he was still very strange but quite well-behaved. He had had a great deal of guilt about an episode in Amsterdam and even surreptitiously returned there to try to find the 'girl' and apologise for using her, despite the fact that he had paid the price she asked. He thought in similar situations that the nuclear war was about to begin.

Antonio saw this as following a situation in which temptation was too great in a man equally strongly racked with guilt. He unraveled much that seemed at first beyond understanding, but in the light of the patient's background, standards and needs became apparently clear. He could often help us in a *poetic* way to grasp the tragedy of mad and powerful impulses in morally terrified people. He helped us to feel it all for ourselves. So one could understand how the end of the world could seem at hand. We all made each other sane and mad. Antonio knew the torment of such a person's soul. He saw our and his need for compassion. Even if we were not totally therapeutically successful, much could be clearly preferable to the vicious circle into which we can so easily slip and so destroy both our chance of any understanding and our patient's whole life and sanity. Antonio also knew that psychodynamic explanations are the guesses we are doomed to make in order to live our day-to-day lives, as well as to be good psychiatrists. They are, however, always precarious hypotheses which must be available for reassessment. They must not be religious tenets.

We often spoke together about the confidence tricks of paradigmatic psychoanalysis.

One mere human being sitting at the end of the couch, the other wretch left believing that totally free revelation of all his thoughts would lead to his rebirth, and of course paying for the privilege. Antonio's scorn was for the arrogance of the analysed, for the belief that peeling each piece of the onion revealed the core. We exchanged notes about the blighted lives of analysts we knew ourselves, comparing many to bald chemists selling hair restorers.

Our discussions took place at parties, in Indian restaurants, in public houses, or in the car on domiciliary visits. The day after a party at my home, to which we had invited several psychotic people, one of the girls was particularly disturbed. I rather crudely asked her to come out for a drink with us as she seemed to have enjoyed the party. Antonio frowned at me. I could see I was to anticipate a rebuke. Antonio later explained: 'You invited her to your house and then you discussed philosophers she had never heard of. You enjoyed your own beneficience. She enjoyed the food, the wine and being included, but perhaps rightly thought even then of tomorrow. Now tomorrow, what has changed in her life? We must be careful of playing with people'. That helped me to say: 'Antonio, I was trying to impress you'. He kindly replied: 'You do'. This was in the context of our repeatedly emphasising how all human beings, including ourselves, have to polish their own images. No other of my twenty-six doctoral students have treated me quite like that.

Perhaps I can be forgiven for seeing his thesis as something of a joint venture, a record in fact of all those parties and debates and of several years of trying to be with the patients. How I would like to achieve as much again, to be so involved in a mutual struggle to achieve some similar mutuality with the patients. Perhaps we will and we do try, but it requires, like nuclear fission, a number of radioactive rods coming together. We had a student, Tim Kendall; an artist, Manuel Chetcuti; Dimitri Vlissides and Jill Hardy with whom Dina and Antonio lived. We had some excellent nurses and beloved patients and my tolerant wife. What halcyon days they were in which the insights in this book developed. I recall no harsh conflicts, just a constant self-reinforcing debate, a rich life of concerts, theatre trips, cooking and curiosity about life itself, especially of how to live it. Why did it inevitably have to end when we had outrageously over-optimistic plans for so much more? Indeed to really understand our schizophrenics. Dear Dina, that made us suffer too, as did seeing your loyal, noble and human attempts to resist the inevitable.

F.A. Jenner, 1989

BIBLIOGRAPHY

Abrams, R., and M.A. Taylor
1982 'The Importance of Schizophrenia Symptoms in the Diagnosis of Mania', *American Journal of Psychiatry* 138: 658-61.

Ajuriaguerra, J.
1954 'Les toubles mentaux au cours des tumeurs de la region meso diencephalique', *Encephale* 5: 406-78.

Alberoni, F.
1983 *Enamoramento e amor* (trans. A. Puga; Amadora: Bertra, n.d.).

Allen, J.E., F.A. Jenner, and J.C. Stevens
1991 'Early Cortical Tactile-Evoked Potentials, Laterality and Schizophrenia', *British Journal of Psychiatry* 158: 529-33.

Asarnow, R.E.
1978 'Residual Performance Deficit in Clinically Remitted Schizophrenics: A Marker for Schizophrenia?', *Journal of Abnormal Psychology* 87: 597-608.

Bachelard, G.
1968 *The Philosophy of No: A Philosophy of the New Scientific Mind* (New York: Orion Press).

Baczko, B.
1985 'Utopia', in *Enciclopedia Einaudi*, V (Lisbon: Imprensa Nacional Casq da Moeda): 333-96.

Baldessarini, R.J.
1985 'Drugs and the Treatment of Psychiatric Disorders', in L.S. Goodman and A. Gilman (eds.), *The Pharmacological Basis of Therapeutic* (New York: Macmillan): 387.

Barber, T.
1969 *A Scientific Approach to Hypnosis* (Princeton: Van Nostrand).

Barthes, R.
1977 *Fragments d'un discours amoreux* (Editions de Seuil, 13; Paris).

Bateson, G.
1978 *Steps to an Ecology of Mind* (New York: Chandler).

Beck, A.T.
1976 *Cognitive Therapy and the Emotional Disorders* (New York: International Universities Press).

Benjamin, L.S.
1976 'Reconsideration of the Kety and Associates: Study of Genetic Factors in the Transmission of Schizophrenia', *American Journal of Psychiatry* 133: 1129-33.

Berlin, I.
1979 *Against the Current: Essays in the History of Ideas* (London: Hogarth Press).

Berrios, G.E.
1981 'Correspondence', *British Journal of Psychiatry* 139: 258-59.

Bertalanffy, L. Von
1968 *General Systems Theory* (New York: Braziller).

Birley, J.L., and G.W. Brown
1970 'Crises and Life Changes Preceding the Onset or Relapse of Acute Schizophrenia: Clinical Aspects', *British Journal of Psychiatry* 116: 327-33.

Bleuler, M.
1950 *Dementia Praecox oder die Gruppe der Schizophrenien* (trans. J. Zinkin; New York: International Universities Press).
1978 *The Schizophrenic Disorders: Long Term and Family Studies* (trans. S.M. Clemens; New Haven: Yale University Press).

Boehme, D.H., *et al.*
1973 'Fluorescent Antibody Studies of Immunoglobulin Binding by Brain Tissues: Demonstration of Cytoplasmic Fluorescence by Direct and Indirect Testing in Schizophrenic and Nonschizophrenic Subjects', *Archives of General Psychiatry* 28: 202.

Bogoch, S.
1960 'Studies on Neurochemistry of Schizophrenic and Affective Disorders', *American Journal of Psychiatry* 116: 743.

Bohr, N.
1976 *Collected Works* (Amsterdam: North Holland Publishing Company).

Bourdillon, R.E., *et al.*
1965 'Pink Spot in the Urine of Schizophrenics', *Nature* 208: 253-71.

Bourdillon, R.E., and A.P. Ridges,
1971 'Catecholamines and Schizophrenia', in H.E. Himwich (ed.), *Biochemistry, Schizophrenias and Affective Illness* (Baltimore: Williams & Wilkins): 123.

Brazier, M., and H. Petsche,
1978 *Architectonics of Cerebral Cortex* (New York: Raven Press).

Bujatti, J., and P. Riederer
1976 'Serotonin, Noradrenalin and Dopamine Metabolites in Transcendental Meditation Techniques', *Neural Transmission* 39: 257.

Bunge, M.
1979 *Causality and Modern Science* (New York: Dover Publications): 353.

Burch, P.R.J., N.R. Rowell and R G. Burwell
1968 'Schizophrenia: Autoimmune or Autoaggressive?', *British Medical Journal* 2: 50.

Campion, L., and G. Tucker
1973 'A Note on Twin Studies, Schizophrenia and Neurological Impairment', *Archives of General Psychiatry* 29: 460-64.

Cancro, R.
1983 'Overview of Schizophrenia', in H.I. Kaplan, A.M. Freedman and B.J. Sadock (eds.), *Comprehensive Textbook of Psychiatry* (London: Williams & Wilkins): 1093-104.

Capra, F.
1976 *The Tao of Physics* (London: Fontana).

Carey, G.
1978 'A Clinical Genetic Study of Obsessional and Phobic States' (PhD thesis, University of Minnesota).

Carlsson, A.
1978 'Antipsychotic Drugs, Neurotransmitters and Schizophrenia', *American Journal of Psychiatry* 135: 165.

Carpenter Jr, W.T., J.S. Strauss and S. Muleh
1973 'Are there Pathognomonic Symptoms in Schizophrenia? An Empiric Investigation of Schneider's First-Rank Symptoms', *Archives of General Psychiatry* 28: 847-52.

Castel, R.
1979 *La société psychiatrique avances* (Paris: Gallimard).
1988 'Il decentramento del sociale', *Per la Salute Mentale* 1: 79-84.

Chadda, R., *et al.*
1986 'HLA Antigens in Schizophrenia-Family Study', *British Journal of Psychiatry* 149: 612.

Chartier, R.
1988 *Historia cultural-entre praticas e representacoes* (trans. M. Manuela Galhardo; Lisbon: Difel).

Chouinard, G., and B.D. Jones
1978 'Neuroleptic-Induced Supersensitivity Psychosis', *American Journal of Psychiatry* 135: 1409-10.

Ciesielski, K.T., H.R. Beech and P.K. Gordon
1981 'Some Electro-Physiological Observations in Obsessional States', *British Journal of Psychiatry* 63: 157.

Ciompi, L.
1980 'The Natural History of Schizophrenia in the Long Term', *British Journal of Psychiatry* 136: 413-20.

Claire, D. St, *et al.*
1989 No Linkage of Chromosome 5 9.11–9.13 Markers to Schizophrenia in Scottish Families', *Nature* 339: 305-309.

Conrad, K.
1957 *Die Beginnende schizophrenie: Versuch einer gestaltanalyse des Wahns* (Stuttgart: Georg Thieme Verlag).

Copley, J.W., A. Guschwan and R.G. Heath
1970 'Serum Creatine Phosphokinase, Aldolase and Copper in Acute and Chronic Schizophrenics', *Biological Psychiatry* 2: 231.

Crow, T.J.
1987 'Neurochemistry and Neuropharmacology of Schizophrenia', in F.A. Henn and E. DeLisi (eds.), *Handbook of Schizophrenia* (Amsterdam: Elsevier): ch. 2.

Cunha-Oliveira, J.A.
1989 'Da inovacao a instituicao e da instituicao a Inovacao (Viagem de Ida-e-Volta Atraves da Psicose)' (Master's thesis, Oporto).

Cunha-Oliveira, J.A., *et al.*
1988 'L'esistente-sofferente e la psicofarmacologia' (communication presented at the II Convegno Internazionale, *La Questione Psichiatrica*); Trieste, Outubro).

Dale, P.W.
1981 'Prevalence of Schizophrenia in the Pacific Island Populations of Micronesia', *Journal of Psychiatric Research* 16: 103-11.

Damas Mora, J., D. Vlissides and F.A. Jenner
1974 'Glucose and Adenosine Triphosphate Level in Normal Subjects', *British Journal of Psychiatry* 125: 459-60.

Dante A.
1921 *Opere di Dante* (Societa Dantesca Italiana: Firenze).

Davies, D.R.
1981 'Exchanges with the Humanities', *Bulletin Royal College of Psychiatrists.*

Day, R.
1981 'Life Events and Schizophrenia: The Triggering Hypothesis', *Acta Psychiatrica Scandinavica* 64: 97-122.

De Clerambault, C.G.
1974 *Themes and Variations in European Psychiatry—An Anthology* (Bristol: John Wright and Sons).

Dell, S.
1980 'Transfer of Special Hospital Patients to the NHS', *British Journal of Psychiatry* 136: 222-34.

Demiisch, L., *et al.*
1977 'Substrate-typic Changes of Platelet Monoamine Oxidase Activity in Subtypes of Schizophrenia', *Archiv fur Psychiatrie und Nervenkrankheiten* 224: 319.

Dewey, J., and A. Bentley
1949 *Knowing and the Known* (Boston: Beacon Press.)

Dilthey, W.
1959 'The Understanding of Other Persons and their Life Expressions', in P. Gardiner (ed.), *Theories of History* (trans. J. Knehl; New York).

Dinnage, R.
1980 'The Story of Ruth', *London Review of Books* 2: 4-17.

Dodds, E.R.
1951 *The Greeks and the Irrational* (Harmondsworth: Pelican Books).

Domino, E.F., and S. Gahagan
1977 'In Vitro Half Life of 14C-Tryptamine in Whole Blood of Drug Free Chronic Schizophrenic Patients', *American Journal of Psychiatry* 134: 1280.

Donahue, D.
1982 'The Arts without Mystery', *The Listener* 11.

Duchamp, M.
1972 *Art Censorship* (Metuchen, NJ: Scarecrow Press).

Egeland, J.A., *et al.*
1987 'Bipolar Affective Disorders Linked to DNA Markers on Chromosome 11', *Nature* 325: 783-87.

Eliade, M.
1952 *Images et symboles* (Paris: Gallimard).
1958 *The Sacred and the Profane* (Chicago: Chicago University Press).

Ellis, A.
1973 *Humanistic Psychotherapy* (New York: Julian Press).

Ey, H.

1963 *Etudes psychiatriques* (Paris: Desclée de Brouwer).

Feldman, M.W., and R.C. Lewoniin

1975 'The Hereditability Hang-up', *Science* 190: 1163-68.

Fischer, M.

1973 'Genetic and Environmental Factors in Schizophrenia', *Acta Psychiatrica Scandinavica* 2381.

Fish, F

1964 'The Historical Development of Modern Psychiatry in Britain and Germany', *Anglo-German Medical Revue* 2: 296-307.

1966 'The Concept of Schizophrenia', *British Journal Medical Psychology* 39: 266-73.

Fitzgerald, B.A., and C.E. Wells

1977 'Hallucinations as a Conversive Reaction', *Disease of the Nervous System* 38: 381-83.

Fonseca, A., and D.A. Fernandes

1965 *Heranca da personalidade: A genetica em psiquiatria* (Porto).

Foucault, M.

1961 *Histoire de la folie à l'age classique* (Paris: Plon).

1963 *Naissance de la clinique* (Paris: Editions Universitaires).

Frankl, V.E.

1963 *Man's Search For Meaning* (Boston: Beacon Press).

1978 *Psychotherapy and Existentialism* (Harmondsworth: Penguin).

Freeman, T.

1981 'On the Psychopathology of Persecutory Delusions', *British Journal of Psychiatry* 139: 529-32

Freeman, T., J.L. Cameron and A. McGhie

1958 *Chronic Schizophrenia* (London: Tavistock Publications).

Freud, S.

1929 *Civilization and its Discontents* (Harmondsworth: Pelican Books).

1932 *Why War?* (Harmondsworth: Pelican Books).

1943 'Psychoanalytische bemerkungen über einen autobiographischen Fall von Paranoia', in *Gesamelte Werke*, VIII (London: Imago Publishing).

Friedhoff, A.F., and E. Van Winkle

1962a 'Isolation and Characterization of a Compound from the Urine of Schizophrenics', *Nature* 194: 879-98.

1962b 'The Characteristics of an Amine Found in the Urine of Schizophrenic Patients', *Journal of Nervous and Mental Diseases* 135: 550.

Furlong, F.W.

1981 'Determinism and Free Will: Review of the Literature', *American Journal of Psychiatry* 138: 435-39.

Gaston, A.

1978 *Genealogia dell'alienazione* (Milan: Feltrinelli).

Gattaz, W.F., *et al.*

1981 'Low Platelet MAO Activity and Schizophrenia: Sex Differences', *Acta Psychiatrica Scandinavica* 64: 167.

Gattaz, W.F., and H. Beckmann,

1981 Platelet MAO Activity and Personality Characteristics', *Acta Psychiatrica Scandinavica* 64: 79.

Gauld, A., and J. Shotter

1977 *Human Action and its Psychological Investigation* (London: Routledge & Kegan Paul).

Gebsattel, V.E. von

1954 *Prologomenu einer Medicinizinischen* (Anthropologie; Berlin: Springer Verlag).

Georgin, B.

1981 'Remarques sur le discours nosologique en psychiatrie: Le nommer ou le dire?', *L'Evolution Psychiatrique* 45: 5-17.

Gershon, E.S.

1981 'The Historical Context of Franz Kallman and Psychiatric Genetics', *Archius der Psychiatrie Nervenkranken* 229: 273-76.

Giddens, A.

1974 *Positivism and Sociology* (London: Heinemann.)

Gjessing, R.

1947 'Biological Investigations in Endogenous Psychose', *Acta Psychiatrica et Neurologica Scandinavica* 47: 93.

Goffman, E.

1961 *Asylums* (Anchor).

1980 *The Presentation of Self in Everyday Life* (Harmondsworth: Pelican Books).

Goodman, N.

1978 *Ways of Worldmaking* (Brighton: Harvester Press).

Gottesman, I.I., and J. Shields

1972 *Schizophrenia and Genetics: A Twin Study Vantage Point* (New York: Academic Press).

Greben, S., and Lesser

1976 'The Essence of Psychotherapy', *British Journal of Psychiatry* 137: 449-55.

Haddon, R.K., and A. Rabe

1963 'An Antigenic Abnormality in the Serum of Chronically Ill Schizophrenic Patients', in R.G. Heath (ed.), *Serological Fractions in Schizophrenia* (New York: Harper & Row), 151.

Haley, J.

1963 *Strategies of Psychotherapy* (New York: Grunne & Stratton).

Hamilton, M.

1985 *Fish's Clinical Psychopathology: Signs and Symptoms in Psychiatry* (Bristol: John Wright & Sons).

Harding, T.

1974 'Serum Creatine Kinase in Acute Psychosis', *British Journal of Psychiatry* 125: 280.

Hare, E.

1979 'Review of Manfred Bleuler's Book', *British Journal of Psychiatry* 135: 474-76.

1988 'Schizophrenia as a Recent Disease', *British Journal of Psychiatry* 153: 521-31.

Hare, E.H.
1974 'The Changing Content of Psychiatric Illness', *Journal of Psychosomatic Research* 18: 283-89.

Harre, R., and P.F. Secord
1972 *The Explanation of Social Behaviour* (Oxford: Basil Blackwell).

Harrow, M., *et al.*
1973 'A Longitudinal Study of Schizophrenic Thinking', *Archives of General Psychiatry* 28: 179-82.

Harrow, M., and D. Quinlan
1977 'Is Disordered Thinking Unique to Schizophrenia?', *Archives of General Psychiatry* 34: 15-21.

Heath, R., and I.M. Krupp
1968 'Schizophrenia as a Specific Biologic Disease', *American Journal of Psychiatry* 124: 1019.

Heidegger, M.
1978 *Being and Time* (trans. J. Macquarrie and E. Robinson; Oxford: Basil Blackwell).

Heimowitz, P., and H. Spohr
1980 'The Effects of Anti-Psychotic Medication on the Linguistic Ability of Schizophrenia', *Journal of Mental and Nervous Disease* 168: 287-96.

Heisenberg, W.I.L.
1962 *Physics and Philosophy of the Revolution in Modern Science* (New York: Harper & Row).

Heller, B., *et al.*
1970 'N-Dimethylated Indoleamines in Blood of Acute Schizophrenics', *Experienta* 26: 503.

Henry, J.P., *et al.*
1971 'Effect of Psychosocial Stimulation on the Enzymes Involved in the Biosynthesis and Metabolism of Noradrenalin and Adrenaline', *Psychosomatic Medicine* 33: 227.

Herder, J.G.
1978 *Gesamteausgabe 1763–1803 unter Leitung von Karl-Heinz Hahn* (Weimar: Bohlaus).

Hesse, M.B.
1974 *The Structure of Scientific Inference* (London: Macmillan).

Heston, L.
1966 'Psychiatric Disorders in Foster Home Reared Children of Schizophrenic Mothers', *British Journal of Psychiatry* 112: 812-25.

Hill, D.
1981 'Mechanisms of Mind: A Psychiatrist's Perspective', *British Journal of Psychology* 54: 1.

Hoffer, A.
1967 'Biochemistry of Nicotine Acid and Nicotinamide', *Psychosomatics* 8: 95.

Hoffman, E., and L. Goldstein
1981 'Hemispheric Quantitative EEG Changes Following Emotional Reactions

in Neurotic Patients', *Acta Psychiatrica Scandinavica* 63: 157.

Holzman, P.S., *et al.*
1977 'Abnormal-Pursuit Eye Movements in Schizophrenia: Evidence for a Genetic Indicator', *Archives of General Psychiatry* 34: 802.
1980 'Deviant Eye Tracking in Twins Discordant for Psychosis', *Archives of General Psychiatry* 37: 627.

Holzman, P.S., L.R. Proctor and D.W. Hughes
1973 'Eyetracking Patterns in Schizophrenia', *Science* 181: 179.

Horrobin, D.F.
1977 'The Roles of Prostaglandins and Prolactin in Depression, Mania and Schizophrenia', *Postgraduate Medical Journal* 53: 160.
1980 'A Singular Solution for Schizophrenia', *New Scientist* 28: 642.

Horrowitz, M.J.
1975 'A Cognitive Study of Hallucination', *American Journal of Psychiatry* 132: 789-95.

Howlett, D.R., and F.A. Jenner
1978 'Studies Relating to the Clinical Significance of Urinary 3-Methoxy-4-Hydroxyphenylethylene Glycol', *British Journal of Psychiatry* 132: 49-54.

Huber, G.
1983 'Das Konzept substratnaher Basissymptome und seine Bedeutung fur Theorie und Therapie schizophrener erkrankungen', *Der Nervenarzt* 54: 23-32.

Huber, G., and R. Schuttler
1975 'A Long Term Follow-up Study of Schizophrenia: Psychiatric Course and Prognosis', *Acta Psychiatrica Scandinavica* 52: 49-57.

Humphrey, M.
1980 'Book Reviews', *British Journal of Psychiatry* 136: 297.

Ingleby, D.
1981 *Critical Psychiatry* (Harmondsworth: Penguin Books).

Iversen, L.
1981 'Lecture to The Royal College of Psychiatrists', Annual Meeting, London.

Jackson, D.D.
1960 'A Critique of the Literature on the Genetics of Schizophrenia', in D.D. Jackson (ed.), *The Etiology of Schizophrenia* (New York: Basic Books), 37.

Jackson, H.
1958 *Selected Writings of Hughlings Jackson* (London: Staple Press).

Jacob, F.
1970 *La logique du vivant* (Paris: Editions Gallimard).

Jacobsen, B., and D.K. Kinney
1980 'Perinatal Complications in Adopted and Nonadopted Schizophrenics and their Controls: Preliminary Results', *Acta Psychiatrica Scandinavica* 62: 337-47.

Jaspers, K.
1963 'Kausale und verstandliche Zusammenhange zwischen Schicksal und Psychose bei der Dementia Praecox (Schizophrenie)', in *Gesammelte Schriften zur Psychpathologie* 14: 158-263.

1968 *General Psychopathology* (trans. J. Hoenig and M.W. Hamilton; Manchester: Manchester University Press).

1968 'The Phenomenological Approach in Psychopathology', *British Journal of Psychiatry* 114: 1313-23.

Jenner, F.A.

1980 Letter to *Middlewood Times*, Sheffield.

1984 'Beyond Complicity and Schizophrenia', *Inscape* (Journal of the British Association of Art Therapists) Winter: 3-6.

Jenner, F.A., and J. Damas-Mora

1983 'Philosophical Reflections on and Neurological Studies of Some Periodic Psychoses', in N. Hatotani and J. Nomura (eds.), *Neurobiology of Periodic Psychoses* (Tokyo: Igaku-Shoin).

Jenner, F.A., and T. Kendall

1991 'Psychiatry and the French Revolution', in D. Williams (ed.), *The Long and the Short of It* (Sheffield: Sheffield Academic Press).

Jenner, F.A., *et al.*

1962 'Bial's Reaction for Neuraminic Acid in Cerebrospinal Fluid from Schizophrenics', *Journal of Mental Science* 108: 822-24.

1975 'Mood and Whole Blood Adenosine Triphosphate', *British Journal of Psychiatry* 127: 478-81.

Jones, H.G.

1971 'In Search of an Ideographic Psychology', *Bulletin of the British Psychological Society* 24: 279-90.

Joyce, J.

1922 *Ulysses* (Paris: Shakespeare Company).

1939 *Finnegans Wake* (London: Faber).

Judkins, M., and P.D. Slade

1981 'A Questionnaire Study of Hostility in Persistant Auditory Hallucinations', *British Journal of Medical Psychology* 54: 243-50.

Kafka, F.

1935 *Der Prozess* (Berlin: Schocken).

Kahlbaum, K.

1874 *Die Katatonie oder das Spannungsirresein* (Berlin: Denticke).

Kallman, F.J.

1938 *The Genetics of Schizophrenia* (New York: J.J. Augustin).

1953 *Heredity in Health and Mental Disorders* (New York: W.W. Norton).

Karlsson, J.L.

1966 *The Biological Basis of Schizophrenia* (Springfield, IL: Charles C. Thomas).

1968 'Genealogic Studies of Schizophrenia' in D. Rosenthal and S.S. Kety (eds.), *The Transmission of Schizophrenia* 85 (London: Pergamon Press).

1970 'Genetic Association of Giftedness and Creativity with Schizophrenia', *Hereditas* 66: 177.

1970 'The Genetics of Schizophrenia and Schizoid Disease', *Science* 167: 249-56.

Kelly, G.

1955 *The Psychology of Personal Constructs* (New York: W.W. Norton).

Kelsoe, J.R., *et al.*
1989 'Re-evaluation of the Linkage Relationship Between Chromosome 11p Loci and the Gene for Bipolar Affective Disorders in the Old Order Armish', *Nature* 392: 238-43.

Kennedy, I.
1980 'The BBC Reith Lectures', *The Listener* 9.

Kennedy, J.L., *et al.*
1988 'Evidence Against Linkage of Schizophrenia to Markers on Chromosome 5 in a Northern Swedish Pedigree', *Nature* 336: 167-70.

Kenny, A.
1976 *Wittgenstein* (Harmondsworth: Pelican Books).

Kety, S.S., *et al.*
1971 'Mental Illness in the Biological and Adoptive Families of Adopted Schizophrenics', *American Journal of Psychiatry* 128: 302-6.

Kety, S.S., and D.K. Kinney
1981 'Biological Risk Factors in Schizophrenia' in D. Regier and G. Allen (eds.), *Risk Factor Research in the Major Mental Disorders,* 41 (Washington D.C.: H.H.S.Pub.No. [ADM]): 81-1068.

Kidd, K.K., and L.L. Cavalli-Storza
1973 'An Analysis of the Genetics of Schizophrenia', *Social Biology* 20: 254-65.

Kierkegaard, S.
1941 *Fear and Trembling* (trans.W. Lowrie; Princeton, NJ: Princeton University Press).

Kinney, D.K.
1983 'Schizophrenia and Major Affective Disorders (Manic-Depressive Illness)', in A.E.H. Emery and D.L. Rimoin (eds.), *Principles and Practice of Medical Genetics* (London: Churchill Livingstone), 321.

Klein, D.F.
1981 'Low Dose Maintenance Treatment of Schizophrenia' (The Royal College of Psychiatrists, Annual Meeting, London).

Koch, H.L.
1966 *Twins and Twin Relations* (Chicago: University of Chicago Press).

Koehler, K.
1979 'First Rank Symptoms of Schizophrenia: Questions Concerning Clinical Boundaries', *British Journal of Psychiatry* 134: 236-48.

Korer, J.
1980 'Phenomenological Psychology and Schizophrenia as Explored by Erwin Strauss', *British Journal of Medical Psychology* 53: 29-35.

Kraepelin, E.
1904 *Psychiatrie* (Leipzig: Johann Ambrosius Barth).

Kretschmer, E.
1918 *Der Sesitive Beziehungswahn* (Berlin: Springer Verlag).

Kringlen, E.
1967 *Heredity and Environment in the Functional Psychoses* (London: Heinemann).

Kubie, L.S.
1971 'Multiple Fallacies in the Concept of Schizophrenia', in Doucet *et al.* (eds.), *Problems of Psychosis* (The Hague: Excerpta Medica): 301-11.
Kuhn, T.
1970 *The Structure of Scientific Revolutions* (Chicago: Chicago University Press).
Lader, M.H.
1975 *The Psychophysiology of Mental Illness* (London: Routledge & Kegan Paul).
Laing, R.D.
1960 *The Divided Self: An Existential Study in Sanity and Madness* (London: Tavistock Publications).
1967 *Conversations with Children* (London: Allen Lane).
Laplace, P.S.
1796 'Exposition du systeme du monde', in *Dictionnaire des citations françaises* (Paris: Robert, 1978).
Leff, J.L., *et al.*
1973 'Life Events and Maintenance Therapy in Schizophrenic Relapse', *British Journal of Psychiatry* 123: 659-60.
Lemert, C.
1979 'Science, Religion and Secularization', *The Sociological Quarterly* 20: 445-61.
Levi-Straus, C.
1966 *The Savage Mind* (Chicago: Chicago University Press).
L'Hermitte, J.
1961 *Les hallucinations: clinique et psychopathologie* (Paris: Desclée de Brouwer).
Lidz, T., S. Blatt and B. Cook
1981 'Critique of the Danish–American Studies of the Adopted-Away Offspring of Schizophrenic Parents', *American Journal of Psychiatry* 138: 1063-68.
Logan, D.G., and S.D. Deodhar
1970 'Schizophrenia, an Immunological Disorder?', *JAMA.* 212: 1703.
Magee, B.
1987 *The Great Philosophers* (Oxford: Oxford University Press).
Mahendra, B.
1973 'Editorial: Where Have All the Catatonics Gone?', *Psychological Medicine* 28: 179-82.
Marcel, G.
1949 *Positions et aproches concretes du mystere ontologique* (Louvain: Nauwelaerts).
Margulies, A., and L.L. Havens
1981 'The Initial Encounter: What to do First?', *American Journal of Psychiatry* 138: 421-28.
Mascari, P.
1979 'Language, Reality and Schizophrenia', *Schizophrenia Bulletin* 5: 334-40.
Mathew, R.J., *et al.*
1981a 'Anxiety and Platelet MAO Levels After Relaxation Training', *American Journal of Psychiatry* 138: 371-73

1981b 'Catecholamines and Monoamine Oxidase Activity in Anxiety', *Acta Psychiatrica Scandinavica* 63: 245.

Matthyssi, S.W., and K.K. Kidd

1976 'Estimating the Genetic Contribution to Schizophrenia', *American Journal of Psychiatry* 133(2): 185.

May, P.R.A.

1971 'Cost Efficiency of Treatments For the Schizophrenic Patient', *American Journal of Psychiatry* 127: 1382-85.

1973 'Rational Treatment for an Irrational Disorder: What Does the Schizophrenic Patient Need?', *American Journal of Psychiatry* 133: 1008-12.

Mazlisch, B.

1966 *The Riddle of History* (New York: McGraw-Hill).

McGlashan, T.H., and W.T. Carpenter

1981 'Does Attitude towards Psychosis Relate to Outcome?', *American Journal of Psychiatry* 138: 797-801.

McGuffin, P., and D. Mawson

1980 'Obsessive-Compulsive Neurosis: Two Identical Twin Pairs', *British Journal of Psychiatry* 137: 285-87.

McKeown, T.

1976 *The Role of Medicine-Dream, Mirage or Nemesis?* (London: Nuffield Provincial Hospital Trust).

McNeill, T.F., and L. Kaij

1978 'Obstetric Factors in the Development of Schizophrenia: Complications in the Births of Preschizophrenics and in Reproduction by Schizophrenic Parents', in L. Wynne, R. Cromwell and S. Matthysse (eds.), *The Nature of Schizophrenia* (New York: Wiley): 401-402.

Mears, A.

1960 *A System of Medical Hypnosis* (New York: Saunders).

Mellet, P.

1980 'Current Views on the Psychophysiology of Hypnosis', *British Journal of Hospital Medicine* May: 441-46.

Mellsop, G., S. Whittingham, and B. Ungar

1973 'Schizophrenia and Autoimmune Serological Reactions', *Archives of General Psychiatry* 28: 194.

Meltzer, H.Y., R. Nunkin and J. Raffery

1971 'Serum Creatine Phosphokinase Activity in Newly Admitted Psychiatric Patients', *Archives of General Psychiatry* 24: 568.

Meltzer, H.Y.

1969 'Muscle Enzyme Release in the Acute Psychoses', *Archives of General Psychiatry* 21: 102.

1976 'Neuromuscular Dysfunction in Schizophrenia', *Schizophrenia Bulletin* 2: 106.

Meltzer, H.Y., and R. Moline

1970a 'Muscle Abnormalities in Acute Psychoses', *Archives of General Psychiatry* 23: 481.

1970b 'Plasma Enzymatic Activity after Exercise: A Study of Psychiatric Patients and their Relatives', *Archives of General Psychiatry* 22: 390.

Mendolson, J.
1964 'Discussion of Dr Fiedhoff's Paper: Biological O-Methylation and Schizophrenia', *Psychiatric Research Reports of American Psychiatric Association* 19: 154.

Merleau-Ponty, M.
1945 *Phenomenologie da la perception* (Paris: Gallimard).

Minkowski, E.
1953 *La schizophrenie: Psychopathologie des schizoids et des schizophrenes* (Paris: Desclée de Brouwer).

Montaigne, M.
1978 *Essais* (ed. J.C. Chapman and F.J.L. Mourett; London: Athlone Press).

Monteiro, A.C.
1983 'The Concepts of Understanding and the Schizophrenia Problem' (PhD Sheffield): 35-48, 58-87, 94-107.

Monteiro, A.C., and J.A.Z. Cardoso
1986 'Que base genetica para a esquizofrenia?', *Rev. Port. Pedag.* 20: 179-201.
1987 'Investigacao neurobiologica e o problema da causalidade na esquizofrenia', *Rev. Port. Pedag.* 21: 119-50.

Moore, M., and H.C. Solomon
1934 'Contributions of Haslam, Bayle, Esmach and Jessen to the History of Neurosyphilis', *Archives of Neurology and Psychiatry* 32: 804-39.

Murphy, H.B.M., and A.C. Raman
1971 'The Chronicity of Schizophrenia in Indigenous Tropical Peoples: Results of a Twelve Year Follow-up Survey in Mauritius', *British Journal of Psychiatry* 118: 489-97.

Murphy, H.B.M., and B.M. Taumorpean
1980 'Traditionalism and Mental Health in the South Pacific: A Re-Examination of an Old Hypothesis', *Psychological Medicine* 10: 471-82.

Needham, J.
1956 'Science and Civilisation', in *China* II: *History of Scientific Thought* (Cambridge: Cambridge University Press).

Nestoros, J.N., T.A. Ban and H.E. Lehmann
1977 'Transmethylation Hypothesis of Schizophrenia: Methionine Nicotinic Acid', *International Journal of Pharmacopsychiatry* 12: 215.

Omond, H., J. Smythies and J. Harley-Mason
1952 'Schizophrenia: A New Approach', *Journal of Mental Science* 98: 309.

Ongaro, B.F.
1982 *Salute/Malattia-le parole della medicina* (Torino: Einaudi).

Orme, M.
1973 *Hypnosis: Research Developments and Perspectives* (London: P. Elek. Scientific Books).

Ortega, J.G.
1957 *The Revolt of the Masses* (New York: Norton).

Pauling, L.
1973 *Orthomolecular Psychiatry, Treatment of Schizophrenia* (San Francisco: W.H. Freeman).

Pieron, H.
1968 *Vocabulaire de la psychologie* (Paris: Presses Universitaires de France).

Pollin, W., P.V. Cardon and S.S. Kety
1961 'Effects of Amino Acid Feedings in Schizophrenic Patients Treated with Iproniazid', *Science* 133: 104.

Pollin, W., and J.R. Stabenau
1968 'Biological, Psychological and Historical Differences in a Series of Monozygotic Twins Discordant for Schizophrenia', in D. Rosenthal and S.S. Kety (eds.), *The Transmission of Schizophrenia* (Oxford: Pergamon Press).

Popper, K.
1963 *Conjectures and Refutations: The Growth of Scientific Knowledge* (London: Routledge & Kegan Paul).

Pulkkinen, E.
1977 'Immunoglobulins, Psychopathology and Prognosis in Schizophrenia', *Acta Psychiatrica Scandinavica* 56: 173.

Rasmussen, S.
1978 'Sensitive Delusion of Reference: Some Reflections on Diagnostic Practice', *Acta Psychiatrica Scandinavica* 58: 441-48.

Read, H.
1955 *Icon and Idea* (Cambridge, MA: Harvard University Press).

Revelly, A., and R. Murray
1980 'The Genetic Contribution to the Functional Psychoses', *British Journal of Hospital Medicine* August: 166-71.

Rickman, H.P.
1967 *Understanding and the Human Studies* (London: Heinemann Educational Books).

Roback, A.
1956 *Present Day Psychology* (London: Allen & Unwin).

Romme, M.A., and A.D. Escher
1989 'Hearing Voices', *Schizophrenia Bulletin* 15: 209-16.

Rose, S., L.J. Kamin and R.C. Lewontin
1984 *Not in our Genes: Biology, Ideology and Human Nature* (Middlesex: Penguin Books).

Rosenberg, D., and G. Tucker
1975 'Computer Content Analysis of Schizophrenic Speech: A Preliminary Report', *American Journal of Psychiatry* 132: 611-16.
1979 'Verbal Behaviour and Schizophrenia', *Archives of General Psychiatry* 36: 1331-37.

Rosenblatt, S., *et al.*
1968 'The Relationship Between Antigamma-Globulin Activity and Depression', *American Journal of Psychiatry* 124: 1640.

Rosenhan, D.I.
1973 'On Being Insane in Insane Places', *Science* 179: 250-58.

Rosenthal, D., *et al.*
1971 'The Adopted-Away Offspring of Schizophrenics', *American Journal of Psychiatry* 128: 307-11.

Rowe, D.
1980 'Philosophy and Psychiatry', *Philosophy* 55: 109-12.

Sachar, E.J.
1970 'Psychological Factors Relating to Activation and Inhibition of the Adrenocortical Stress Response in Man: A Review', *Progress in Brain Research* 32: 316.

Sampaio-Bruno
1983 *O encoberto* (Porto: Lollo and Tama).

Sartre, J.P.
1943 *L'etre et le neant* (Paris: Gallimard).

Scharfetter, C.
1980 *General Psychopathology* (London: Cambridge University Press).
1981 'Ego-Psychopathology: The Concept and its Empirical Evaluation', *Psychological Medicine* 11: 273-80.

Schatzman, M.
1980 *The Story of Ruth* (London: Duckworth).

Scheridan, A.
1980 *Michel Foucault—The Will to Truth* (London: Tavistock Publications).

Schneider, K.
1955 *Psychopathologia Clinique* (trans. J. Plegrand; Lovain: Nauwelaerts).
1959 *Clinical Psychopathology* (trans. M. Hamilton; London: Grumme & Stretton).

Schweid, D.E., J.S. Steinberg and H. Sudak
1972 'Creatine Phosphokinase and Psychosis', *Archives of General Psychiatry* 26: 263.

Scull, A. (ed.)
1981 *Mad Houses, Mad Doctors and Madmen—The Social History of Psychiatry in the Victorian Era* (London: Athlone Press).

Shagass, C., M. Amadeo and D.A. Overton
1974 'Eye-tracking Performance in Psychiatric Patients', *Biological Psychiatry* 9: 245.

Shagass, C., R.A. Roemer and M. Amadeo
1976 'Eye-tracking Performance and Engagement of Attention', *Archives of General Psychiatry* 33: 121.

Sherington, R., *et al.*
1988 'Localisation of a Susceptibility Locus for Schizophrenia on Chromosome 5', *Nature* 336: 161-67

Shields, J., L.L. Heston and I.I. Gottesman
1975 'Schizophrenia and the Schizoid: The Problem for Genetic Analysis', in R.R. Fieve, D. Rosenthal and H. Brill (eds.), *Genetic Research in Psychiatry* (Baltimore: Johns Hopkins University Press).

Silverstone, M.L., and M. Harrow
1981 'Schneiderian First-Rank Symptoms in Schizophrenia', *Archives of General Psychiatry* 38: 288-93.

Singer, J.
1975 *The Inner World of Daydreaming* (New York: Harper & Row).

Slade, P.D.
1973 'The Psychological Investigation and Treatment of Auditory Hallucinations: A Second Case Report', *British Journal of Medical Psychology* 46: 293-96.

Slater, E., and V.A. Cowie
1969 *Studies of Anxiety* (Ashford: Headley Brothers).
1971 *The Genetics of Mental Disorders* (London: Oxford University Press).

Smith, A.
1980 'Adoption Research in Schizophrenia', *Correspondence, British Journal of Psychiatry* 136: 352.

Smith, K., and J.O. Sines
1960 'Demonstration of a Peculiar Odour in the Sweat of Schizophrenic Patients', *Archives of General Psychiatry* 20: 272.

Smythies, J .R.
1963 *Schizophrenia: Chemistry, Metabolism and Treatment* (Springfield: Charles C. Thomas).

Solomon, G.F., *et al.*
1969 'Immunoglobulins in Psychiatric Patients', *Archives of General Psychiatry* 20: 272.

Spinoza, B.
1962 *Ethics* (London: Dent).

Stabenau, J.R., W. Polin and L. Mosher
1968 'Serum Macroglobulin (S19) in Families of Monozygotic Twins Discordant for Schizophrenia', *American Journal of Psychiatry* 125: 309.

Stacey, M.
1979 'New Perspectives in Clinical Medicine: The Sociologist', *Journal of the Royal College of Physicians of London* 13: 123-29.

Stierlin, H.
1967 'Bleuler's Concept of Schizophrenia: A Confusing Heritage', *American Journal of Psychiatry* 123: 996-1001.

Stoffels, H.
1975 'The Problem of Objectivity in Medicine', *The Human Context* 7: 517-29.

Stone, A., and S. Eldred
1959 'Delusional Formation during the Activation of Chronic Schizophrenic Patients', *Archives of General Psychiatry* 1: 177-79.

Stone, E.A., K.A. Bonnett and M.A. Hofer
1976 'Survival and Development of Maternally Deprived Rats: Role of Body Temperature', *Psychosomatic Medicine* 38: 242.

Sullivan, H.S.
1931 'Socio-Psychiatric Research', *American Journal of Psychiatry* 10: 987-88.

Szasz, T.
1970 *The Manufacture of Madness: A Comparative Study of the Inquisition and the Mental Health Movement* (New York: Harper & Row).

1971 *The Manufacture of Madness* (London: Routledge & Kegan Paul).
1976 *Schizophrenia—The Sacred Symbol of Psychiatry* (New York: Basic Books).

Tarrier, N., *et al.*
1979 'Bodily Reactions to People and Events in Schizophrenics', *Archives of General Psychiatry* 36: 311-15.

Teixeira de Pascoaes
1984 San Paulo (Lisboa: Assirio & Alvim).

Toone, B.K., E. Cooke and M.H. Lader
1981 'Electrodermal Activity in the Affective Disorders and Schizophrenia', *Psychological Medicine* 11: 497.

Totman, R.
1979 *Social Causes of Illness* (London: Souvenir Press).

Turner, W.G.
1979 'Genetic Markers for Schizophrenia', *Biological Psychiatry* 14: 177.

Turner, W.J., and H.E. Chipps
1966 'A Heterophil Menolysin in Human Blood: Distribution in Schizophrenics and Non-Schizophrenics', *Archives of General Psychiatry* 15: 373.

Van den Berg, J.H.
1982 'On Hallucinating: Critical-Historical Overview and Guidelines for Future Study', in A.J.J. de Koning and F.A. Jenner (eds.), *Phenomenology and Psychiatry* (London: Academic Press).

Vaughn, C., and J.P. Leff
1979 'The Influence of Family and Social Factors on the Course of Psychiatric Illness: A Comparison of Schizophrenic and Depressed Neurotic Patients', *British Journal of Psychiatry* 129: 125-37.

Veith, J.
1965 *Hysteria: The History of a Disease* (Chicago: University of Chicago Press).

Venables, P., and J.K. Wing
1962 'Level of Arousal and the Subclassification of Schizophrenia', *Archives of General Psychiatry* 7: 114-19.

Vico, G.
1970 *The New Science* (London: Carnell University Press).

Vlissides, D.N., A. Venulet and F.A. Jenner
1986 'A Double-Blind Gluten-Free/Gluten-Load Controlled Trial in a Secure Ward Population', *British Journal of Psychiatry* 148: 447-52.

Wagner, R.
1976–77 'The Relationship Between Language and Disease Concept', *International Journal of Psychiatric Medicine* 7: 42-40.

Weiner, H.
1983 'Schizophrenia: Etiology', in H.I. Kaplan, A.M. Freedman and B.J. Sadock (eds.), *Comprehensive Textbook of Psychiatry*, III (London: Williams & Wilkins): 1121-52.

Whittingham, S., *et al.*
1968 'Absence of Brain Antibodies in Patients with Schizophrenia', *British Medical Journal* 1: 347.

Whorf, B.L.
1964 *Language, Thought and Reality* (Cambridge: Massachusetts Institute of

Technology Press).

Wijsenbeck, H., *et al.*
1980 'Single Case Study: Conversive Hallucinations', *Journal of Nervous and Mental Diseases* 168: 564-65.

Wing, J.K.
1978 *Reasoning About Madness* (Oxford: Oxford University Press).
1978 'The Social Context of Schizophrenia', *American Journal of Psychiatry* 135: 1333 .

Wing, J.K., J.E. Cooper and N. Sartorius
1973 *Present State Examination* (Cambridge: Cambridge University Press).

Wittgenstein, L.
1976 *Philosophical Investigations* (trans. G.E.M Anscombe; Oxford: Basil Blackwell).

Wolkind, S. (ed.)
1979 *Medical Aspects of Adoption and Foster Care* (Spastic International Medical Publications with Heinemann Medical).

World Health Organisation (WHO)
1973 *The International Pilot Study of Schizophrenia* (Geneva).

Wyatt, R.J., *et al.*
1975 'Low Platelet Monoamino Oxidase and Vulnerability to Schizophrenia', in E.J. Mendlewicz (ed.), *Modern Problems Of Pharmaco-Psychiatry: Genetics and Psychopharmacology* (Karger S, 10: Basel): 38.

Zubin, J., and B. Spring
1977 'Vulnerability—A New View of Schizophrenia', *Journal of Abnormal Psychiatry* 86: 103-26.

AUTHOR INDEX